SECRETS OF DYNAMIC
COMMUNICATION

*Preparing and Delivering
Powerful Speeches*

KEN DAVIS

Christian Life Educators Network (CLEN) is a world-wide network of member schools in affiliation with CLST Global. CLEN offers complete support services to member schools and students. Through an articulation agreement with CLST Global, students in CLEN schools can earn CLST Global Certificates, Diplomas and Degrees.

Christian Life School of Theology Global (CLST Global) has met the requirements for exemption from applicable Georgia law as a religious institution under the provision of the Post-secondary Educational Authorization Act, Georgia Code 20-3-100 et seq. As a result, CLST Global awards a variety of Ministry Certificates, Diplomas and Degrees ranging from an Associate of Theology through a Doctor of Sacred Studies.

This book is dedicated to all the men and women who faithfully proclaim the Good News of Christ.

How beautiful are the feet of those who bring good news!
Romans 10:15

Contents

Contents

Acknowledgments

I wish to give special thanks to the people who have made the publication of this book possible.

To my wife Diane, for the hours of trying to decipher my writing, printing dozens of manuscripts, and enduring stressful behavior that intensified as the deadline drew near.

To Candie Blankman for the research and outline that were invaluable contributions to chapter 8 and the wise counsel that affected every chapter.

To Kathy Colebank who can spot theological inconsistencies and poor sentence structure at 1,000 paces and is not afraid to point them out.

To Jim Green for his constant challenge to excellence during the development of SCORRE and his contribution to the chapter on illustrations.

To Byron Emmert for his involvement in Dynamic Communicators Workshops and his influence on many of the concepts presented in this book.

To Haddon Robinson and Lloyd Perry for the inspiration of their excellent books on biblical preaching.

Introduction

When an author submits a book for publication, one of the first questions an editor asks is "Who is this book written for?" I wrote *Secrets of Dynamic Communication* with a wide variety of people in mind. If you are included in one of the groups below, continue reading because you are going to find this book a valuable resource. If you are not listed, keep reading anyway, I may have missed the special niche that you occupy.

Whether you speak only on rare occasions or find yourself addressing an audience every day, this book is for you. It will be beneficial to the experienced pro as well as the new beginner.

Career pastors, youth workers, and other professional speakers will find help in assessing their effectiveness and practical tools for sharpening their skills.

Students in public speaking courses and seminaries will find practical application of the theory they are learning. The book will help them prepare and deliver powerful speeches confidently without extensive experience.

Sunday school teachers, youth sponsors, leaders of women's groups, committee chairpersons, and anyone else who is called upon to speak and wants to do it with excellence will find this book invaluable.

I have written primarily for those who communicate the greatest message on the face of the earth, the gospel of Jesus Christ, but the principles taught here work just as well for public speakers with secular messages. Executives, sales personnel, and after-dinner speakers can glean much from this book too.

You won't find abstract theories here, only step-by-step help in preparing and delivering speeches that get results. The book will enable you to focus your efforts and organize your material so that you can approach your delivery with confidence and power. It will provide you with ideas and suggestions for enhancing your communication. You'll develop the dynamic speaking skills usually associated with the very best speakers.

You won't find magic formulas or gimmicks here either. In fact, you'll come to see that the secrets of dynamic communication need not be secrets at all. You'll discover principles that have been tested and proved by hundreds of speakers all over the world, principles that will work also for you.

If you have read this far, then this book is definitely written for you. As you benefit from it, please share it with others, especially those entrusted with proclaiming the Good News.

Chapter One

THE MOST IMPORTANT INGREDIENT

THE NEED FOR FOCUS

The most important ingredient in effective communication is a well-kept secret. If I were to ask you what that ingredient was, what would your answer be? Humor? Voice inflection? Interesting material? Good illustrations? Dynamic personality? All of these contribute to the skills of a good speaker, but the most important ingredient to dynamic communication is *focus*. Whether you are a pastor, youth worker, Sunday school teacher, or public speaker, if you want people to listen, learn, and take action, you must speak with crystal-clear focus.

Shortly before I was graduated from high school, I was invited to go deer hunting with the men from our church. Because we were a small farming community without much income, we depended heavily on this hunt to feed the families in our congregation. I had dreamed of this honor for years, and I can still feel the excitement of that frosty November morning.

I had hiked less than a hundred yards into the forest when a shot rang out. The bullet from that shot hit a tree only inches from my face and the splattering bark left welts on my cheek. My mind calculated the available data and concluded: "That *was* close."

I had taken only a few more steps when the second shot zipped above my head. As bits of leaf and branch landed on my shoulders my mind once again considered the data and concluded: "That was close!"

The third shot followed almost immediately and came so close to my ear that I felt heat as it passed. This time my mind quickly screamed its terrifying conclusion: "Someone is shooting at you!"

I dived for the ground as shot after shot buzzed above my head. From my new position I could see the man who had done the shooting. He had used up all his ammunition and was in the process of reloading his gun. Since I hadn't used any of my bullets I managed to convince him that it would be hazardous to his health to shoot at me again.

This dangerous person should not have been allowed out of his pickup. What he lacked was focus. Evidently his philosophy of hunting was, "There are deer in the woods somewhere. If I just pump enough lead in there, I'm bound to get one."

This is a dangerous and ineffective hunting strategy. It is also an ineffective communication strategy, yet I am convinced that it is the unconscious, unspoken approach of many Christian communicators. "There are people out there somewhere," they reason. "If we just pump enough information in their direction, we're bound to hit somebody."

Nothing could be further from the truth. It doesn't matter how fancy your gun or silver your bullets. It doesn't even matter how good a shot you are. If you don't aim at *some-thing* you will hit *nothing*.

Furthermore, if *you* have no focused objective for your talk, how can you expect *the audience* to know what you are talking about? In the first few moments of your speech the audience is deciding whether you have any-thing important to say. If they discern that there is no direction or focus to your talk, you might as well pack your bags and go home because that's what their minds will do.

Those who communicate the Good News of Christ often end up preparing ineffectual shotgun messages. Desperately wanting something—anything—to get through to their audiences, they try to say it all and end up communicating nothing. Some even believe that they can be more effective if they demonstrate their total knowledge of a subject by cramming as much as possible into the time available. These misconceptions have left a communication gap that can be filled only by the power of focused speaking.

Several years ago we did a survey of 2,500 people leaving church services, youth meetings, conventions, and con-ferences. Although the survey was conducted less than fifteen minutes after the message, over 70 percent of the people leaving those meetings had no idea what had been communicated. Of the remaining 30 percent, some could remember a joke or illustration, but most couldn't identi-fy any purpose or direction for the talk.

But that isn't the sad statistic. We also interviewed the speakers and discovered that more than 50 percent of them could not articulate in a simple sentence any objective or focus to their talk. No wonder the audience didn't get anything!

That's why a dynamic presentation is secondary to focus. What good is it to be dynamic if no one can tell what you are dynamic about? What good are illustrations that go nowhere or interesting material that ends up on a dead-end street. Dynamics and theatrics without focus is only entertainment. Certainly there is a time and a place for that, but if you want to communicate, the single most important ingredient is focus.

THE CONSEQUENCES OF UNFOCUSED COMMUNICATION

If you don't set a focus, an unconscious one will take over.

Several years ago, a youth director in Tampa asked speaker Jim Green to address his youth group. When Jim asked whether there was any special objective for the evening, the youth director replied, "It really doesn't matter what you talk about so long as you fill about a half hour." The unconscious objective that took over in this case was simply to fill the allotted time. It would be easy to criticize this young man for the lack of direction in his planning. Yet how many times have you found yourself preparing with no other objective than that a meeting is coming and you must come up with a message?

Jim encouraged the youth director to develop a specific objective for the evening. After some thought he concluded that his kids desperately needed to be encouraged in

discipleship. He asked Jim to focus his talk on the importance of discipleship and to encourage the kids to get involved in a discipleship class. Jim prepared his message with that focus.

Jim called me after his presentation. It was the first message he had delivered using the methods taught in this book. When I asked him how it went, his response revealed the power of focused communication. He said, "The kids didn't laugh so much as before." At first this seemed like discouraging news. He wasn't so funny because he had left out many of his humorous stories that didn't contribute to the objective of his talk. "But when I was finished," Jim continued, "eighteen teenagers walked right past the refreshment table (a modern-day miracle in itself) and signed up for the discipleship class." Now, *that* is communication!

If you don't pinpoint your objective, unconscious objectives such as "I just need to fill the allotted time" will drain the power from your presentations.

Other vague, power-stealing objectives that will rear their heads are:

> I hope they like me.
> I want to give a lot of information.
> I must get through this entire chapter.
> I hope they are impressed with the depth of my knowledge.
> I must cover every item on the agenda.
> I have to make a good impression.

This concept was graphically illustrated on one of my hunting trips. I hung up my guns many years ago to hunt with a bow and arrow. I practiced until I was able to put all my arrows in an apple at twenty yards, and on several occasions I even split arrows because I was shooting them so close together. The only way to achieve that kind of accuracy is to concentrate on one tiny spot right in the center of the bull's-eye. I worked at this concentration until I could hit a tennis ball rolling across the ground.

One day while hunting, I peeked over a ridge to discover one of the biggest bucks I had ever seen, standing ten yards away and completely unaware of my presence. With horns that looked like trees, this deer was every hunter's dream. To be successful I had to shoot an arrow in an area about the size of a paper plate just behind the front shoulder. There was no way I could miss. At this range I could hit a fifty-cent piece every time. I was still amazed at the size of his horns as I pulled back the bow and released the arrow and hit the deer...*right in the horns!* Instead of picking a tiny spot to aim at, I had unconsciously concentrated on the horns. That deer is probably still roaming the woods today telling his grandchildren about this crazy guy with a sharp stick that couldn't hit the broad side of a barn.

I had forgotten to focus on a pinpointed objective, and an unconscious objective had taken over.

In my early days of youth ministry my unconscious objective was "I hope they like me." I was trying to communicate the gospel, but because I was unfocused in my preparation I was hitting the horns instead. My unconscious objective was met. They did like me, but I wasn't communicating well.

One night, I overheard a conversation between two students who had just left one of my presentations. When the first student arrived to pick up the second he asked, "What did you think of the speaker tonight?"

The second student replied, "Oh, he was great."

"What did he say?" the first student inquired.

Without hesitation the second responded, "I don't know, but he was sure good."

Good at what? Good at entertaining maybe, but certainly not good at communication.

In one of our surveys we interviewed a member of the audience who had just attended a message by a well-known speaker. Our first survey question was, "What did you think of the speaker?" With a smile the woman replied, "He was really deep." Our second question was, "What did he say?" After a short pause she responded, "He said really deep stuff."

Further questioning revealed that this woman could not remember even one of those deep concepts he had communicated. This is of particular concern because the interview took place less than five minutes after his presentation. I happened to be in that meeting and the speaker did articulate some deep concepts. In fact he unloaded about fifteen deep concepts. This woman's mind went on overload near the very beginning of his talk and as a result he impressed her with his knowledge rather than successfully imparting some of that knowledge to her. How much more effective he would have been if he had focused on *one* of those concepts and allowed his audience to comprehend it.

I believe this is one of the reasons why so many people say, "Our teacher [youth leader/pastor] is really good but the messages don't apply to me." It's not always expressed in those exact words, but the general idea is the same. No one is excited about just receiving a pile of information. That kind of "cognitive dump" leaves the audience with no handles for application, or it simply overloads the circuits and leaves the listener admiring the intellect of the speaker.

THE METHOD FOR ACHIEVING FOCUS

The sculptor who conceives a beautiful image she wishes to share with the public begins with a solid hunk of granite. All of the granite is good granite, yet to bring the image to life she must start chipping away perfectly good granite. Only by getting rid of what doesn't contribute to the image is she able to bring that image to the public. The same is true when preparing a speech or sermon. To make it as clear and powerful as possible it is necessary to leave out perfectly good material if it doesn't contribute to the objective.

Haddon Robinson says,

> A sermon should be a bullet and not a buckshot. Ideally each sermon is the explanation, interpretation, or application of a single dominant idea supported by other ideas, all drawn from one passage or

several passages of Scripture. (*Biblical Preaching* [Baker, 1980], 33)

This "bullet" principle applies to all kinds of speaking.

Speaking with an objective is essential to good communication. All good books on communication agree with Robinson's point. The question is, how does a speaker achieve this focus? The *sculptor* uses a chisel. *Hunters* use a scope that shuts out all but the tiny area that the hunter wishes to hit. It draws his attention to a minute point of focus right where two small lines cross. But what does a speaker use as a scope?

In the next chapter, you will learn about a method for preparing messages that, like a scope, forces the speaker to an absolute pinpointed focus. The preparation method is called SCORRE. The two primary functions of the SCORRE process are the following:

1. It will serve as a *scope* to help you focus on a single objective just as the scope on a gun blocks out all but the very center of the target.

2. It will provide you with a logical framework so you can construct a bullet of truth that will not miss.

Here is a brief overview of how SCORRE accomplishes those goals. SCORRE is an acronym. The S stands for subject, the C for central theme, the O for objective, the R for rationale, the second R for resources, and the E for evaluation (see Figure 1).

The Most Important Ingredient

S = Subject
C = Central Theme
O = Objective
R = Rationale
R = Resources
E = Evaluation

Figure 1

Establishing a *subject* and choosing a single aspect of that subject as a *central theme* is the very beginning of the focusing process. It helps the speaker zero in on what he or she wants to *talk about* and keeps the speaker from talking about too much. You can see from the illustration of the hourglass (Figure 2) that this part of the process narrows down the broader possibilities and aims the speech in a specific direction.

Figure 2

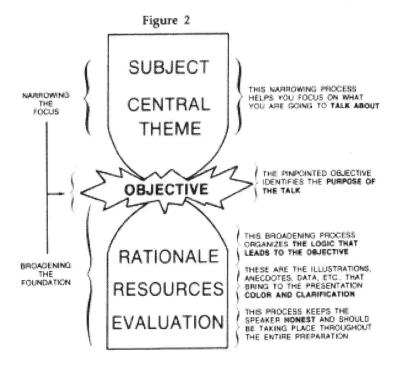

Writing the *objective* in a single sentence forces the speaker to consider the single purpose of the message. When the *speaker* clearly understands the objective of the talk, the likelihood of effective communication increases considerably.

You will learn to write an *objective* sentence that articulates the pinpoint focus of your speech. There should be only one objective for each talk.

Building a powerful *rationale* provides the logical framework for persuasion or encouragement. The *rationale* should lead the listener to your objective. Just as choosing the subject and central theme narrows the focus to a single objective, the rationale is a broadening process that builds a base of organized material to support your objective (see Figure 2 again).

Resources continue to broaden the presentation by bringing color to the talk that will keep the listener interested. Resources personalize what might otherwise seem like abstract ideas and may also include data or illustrations that support what is presented in your rationale.

Evaluation is a process of self-examination. It causes the speaker to ask repeatedly, "Do I know what I am talking about?" and keeps him or her focused on the objective for the talk and its effectiveness in reaching the audience.

REVIEW

You should commit a few key facts to memory before you move on to the next chapter. The following review is designed to help you.

1. What are the two primary functions of the SCORRE process?

   a. It serves as a scope to help the speaker focus on a single _____.

   b. It serves as a _____ framework allowing the speaker to construct a bullet of truth that will not miss.

2. Do the *subject* and *central theme* part of the process serve to narrow or broaden the possibilities for material? _____.

3. The *subject* and *central theme* will represent what the speaker wants to _____ _____.

4. The *objective* pinpoints the _____ of the talk.

5. The *rationale* are the points of _____ that will lead to the objective.

6. The *resources* bring _____ to the talk.

7. The *evaluation* gives the speaker an opportunity to assess the talk's effectiveness in reaching the _____.

Answers: 1. a. *objective* 1. b. *logical* 2. *narrow* 3. *talk about* 4. *purpose* 5. *logic* 6. *color* 7. *audience*

Chapter Two

THE SCORRE PROCESS—SUBJECT AND CENTRAL THEME

Everything I say reminds me of something else.
Lowell Thomas

I believe so strongly in the power of focus, I am convinced that any concerted effort to keep a speech confined to a single objective will dramatically improve communication, even if that is the only effort made. I am equally convinced that the lack of such effort does more to destroy communication than any other single factor.

Several years ago in Alaska I saw this principle demonstrated in a unique way. I visited a remote hunting camp powered by electricity generated from a stream so small you could step across it. The owner had narrowed the stream at one point to about eighteen inches and placed a paddle wheel there. The wheel powered a generator which in turn provided electricity for the entire camp. Two years later I returned to find the camp had been destroyed. The stream had flooded its banks. When the water was focused and controlled, it had provided power for the entire complex, but the uncontrolled rambling of the same stream brought only destruction.

I once spent a delightful evening listening to the late Lowell Thomas speak at a benefit. It soon became obvious that it would be an evening of entertainment rather than instruction or motivation. Mr. Thomas paused at one point and acknowledged the powerful temptation to ramble. "Forgive me," he chuckled, "but everything I say reminds me of something else."

Well said. At best, the temptation to ramble is difficult to resist. Without proper preparation, it is impossible.

The words on this page are not what I wrote originally. What you are reading was at one time two pages. It was only after rewriting five or six times and having the editor trim the final bits of unnecessary fat that it was focused enough for your reading.

I wanted to include a hilarious illustration of the angel and the worm not because it would contribute to the objective of this book but because it was so clever. You, too, will want to present all the results of your study or research simply because it seems too good to waste and took too much time to discover. Remember that you can always save them for another time.

Deep down, every speaker has a desire to keep the scope of the presentation focused and powerful, yet few know how to prepare to achieve that focus. So how does one resist the temptation to ramble and prepare a talk that will hit the mark? That is what the core of this book is all about. Those few speakers who know how are recognized as powerful and persuasive communicators. Not all of them use the methods described in this book, but to the last one they all have some method that keeps them focused and organized.

The method described in this chapter is one that you can grasp quickly and use as a tool to chip away unnecessary granite so that a clear image reaches your audience. It will never be a comfortable process because it forces you to resist the natural urge to wander.

I would like to suggest that the best way to read this material is to prepare a simple speech as you go. You will immediately experience the frustration of forcing yourself to a single focus, but if you stick with it, you will also begin to see the power that comes with such a discipline. Although this process works with all kinds of speeches, it is wise to start with a simple topical speech. Later chapters will detail how the SCORRE system works to prepare everything from a report to an expository sermon, but keep it simple at first. With that in mind grab a pencil and let's move ahead.

CHOOSE A SUBJECT

The first step in preparing a focused speech is to choose a single subject from the endless possibilities available. This may sound overly simplistic, yet every year I hear hundreds of speeches and sermons that attempt to cover several subjects.

Your subject should be expressed in one or two words. Make the words broad enough to include what you want to talk about yet narrow enough to avoid a description of your entire talk.

If you plan to talk about how to ride a horse, "horseback riding" is your subject. "How to ride a horse" might be your central theme, but it is too narrow for your subject. If you plan to give an account of your skindiving trip to the Bahamas, "skindiving" is your subject. If you wish to encourage your audience to follow the commands of Christ to love each other, "love" is your subject.

Starting with a broad subject makes it easier to organize your thoughts as you focus your speech. It also makes it easier to determine the objective of your talk when you are not sure at first what that objective might be. Here are some examples of possible subjects: love, fear, prayer, rabies, abortion, morality, horses.

Before you choose your subject consider these guidelines.

1. The subject must touch your audience.

I once sat in on a Sunday school class of several hundred teenagers. I was shocked to see that many in this class were crying. A few discreet questions revealed that two teenagers who attended that class had been killed in an auto accident during the week. The leader opened his book to the lesson for the morning and barreled ahead, missing the desperate needs expressed by his audience.

It is essential to make contact with the audience if you expect to communicate. You have made contact when the audience perceives that what you are saying applies to them. This holds true whether you are preaching, teaching, or making a presentation on your trip to some exotic location. If the audience doesn't sense a need to hear what you are saying, you may as well talk to an empty room.

As you prepare, consider the needs of your audience. At the very least, the subject must be of interest to them or you must present it in such a manner that it will capture their interest. We will discuss ways to accomplish this in a later chapter.

2. The subject must be within the bounds of your knowledge.

   Do you know what you are talking about?

Shortly after I began my public speaking career I was asked to speak to the sales force of a well-known company. I quickly scanned several books on sales techniques and prepared a speech that would give them the best of what each of these authors had to offer. The problem was I didn't know what I was talking about, I was only repeating the words that others had written.

Actually, the speech went quite well until one of the men raised his hand and asked a question. Since my knowledge didn't go any deeper than the words I was saying, I was caught in my ignorance. It was one of the most embarrassing moments of my life. I should have spent more time studying or stayed with a more familiar subject.

The more intimately you know your subject, the more enthusiastic your presentation will be. The more enthusiastic your presentation, the better it will be received.

Have you ever listened to a pianist who played mechanically, without feeling? All the notes are right, but you soon lose interest. Most of the time the music is played without feeling because the musician is concentrating too much on technique. The pianist who has practiced for years and intimately knows her music is free to play with the expression that captures people's hearts. In the same way, the speaker who knows his subject is free to deliver his message with power.

Do you live what you are talking about?

The one ingredient that will bring sparkle to any talk is the unshakable commitment of the speaker to the truth being presented. The enthusiasm of a salesperson who believes in his product gives him a persuasive edge that can never be duplicated in a canned sales talk. Likewise, if you live daily in the forgiving love of Jesus Christ, it will bring power and longevity to your ministry. When you practice what you preach, you preach better.

3. The subject may be limited by assignment.

Sometimes a speaker doesn't have the advantage of choosing a familiar subject. Pastors get their messages from the exposition. Youth leaders may be committed to following a lesson plan. Others may be asked to deliver a speech on a special topic. Such situations require enough time to study even if you must postpone your presentation until you are ready.

4. The subject may be limited by the intent of Scripture.

Whenever you are teaching or preaching from Scripture, it is of utmost importance that you be true to the truth presented in the text. You should always approach Scripture to find the truth rather than to support preconceived ideas. We will discuss this in detail in another chapter. For now it is enough to say that the Scriptures will contain their own subject; if you are going to preach or teach directly from a passage of Scripture, you must draw your subject from that text.

FOCUS IN ON A CENTRAL THEME

Step two in the focusing process is to choose a *single aspect* of your subject as a central theme. The central theme must be brief and crystal clear. The purpose for choosing a central theme is to narrow the content of the talk to a manageable amount of specific information. This keeps the speaker from covering too much and makes the talk more interesting and relevant.

Using the examples of the subjects mentioned above, here are central themes you could develop.

Skindiving

> The thrills of skindiving
>
> The dangers of skindiving
>
> How to skindive safely
>
> How to learn to skindive
>
> Places to skindive
>
> How to make money skindiving

Even though the subject of skindiving seems narrow to start with, each of these central themes represent one aspect of skindiving. Some are more narrow than others and any one of them would be more powerful than a speech that tried to cover the entire subject.

Love

This subject is so broad that we don't have room to list all of the possible central themes. It might be possible to give a general talk on all aspects of skindiving, although I would never recommend it. The subject of love is also far too broad for such a speech, yet I have heard dozens of unfocused attempts to do just that. It was obvious in each case that what the speaker really wanted was to emphasis a single aspect of love, but the lack of focus made the temptation to ramble irresistible. These speakers wandered because they had not disciplined themselves to decide on their focus by choosing a central theme.

Here are just a few of the possible central themes you could develop from the subject of love.

How to show love to your neighbor

Why you should love your neighbor

How to show love to a spouse

The kinds of love

The love of God

How to show love to God

Loving your children

Loving your parents

How to accept love from others

God's definition of love

The process of choosing a central theme may lead you to reconsider your choice of a subject. For example one of my students chose the subject "vacationing." As he analyzed his central theme it became obvious that he wanted to talk about the thrills of skindiving. Once his focus was clear he realized that his talk really had little to do with vacationing. He wasn't going to give any information on how to choose a vacation or why vacationing is important. He simply wanted to share the thrills of the sport of skindiving. He had put down vacationing as his subject because he happened to go skindiving on his vacation. Changing his subject to skindiving helped him focus his own thoughts and kept him from straying from his subject.

You should be open to this kind of refinement until all the elements of your talk are crystal clear. As you define your objective and rationale you may find it necessary to go back again and adjust the subject and central theme to express your focus more accurately.

It is important to remember that choosing a subject and central theme are the elementary building blocks for developing a speech. As you grow more comfortable with the process you may skip these steps. After many years of using this method, I usually go immediately to the objective as I begin my preparation. Yet when I run into difficulty it is always helpful to go back to these basics. Until you are familiar with the process always start by choosing a subject and central theme.

Examples of possible central themes with their corresponding subjects

Prayer
Roadblocks to Prayer
Place to Pray
Attitudes of Prayer
The Power of Prayer
The Reason of Prayer

Fear
Overcoming Imagined Fears
Facing Fear
Identifying Real Fear
The Objects of Fear
Fear of God

Christ
The Life of Christ
The Deity of Christ
The Teachings of Christ
Knowing Christ
The Humanity of Christ

Communication
The Demands of Communication
Styles of Communication
Communication with God
The Essentials of Communication
Communication With Confidence

Relationships
Building Relationships
Family Relationships
Inter-church Relationships
Healing Broken Relationships
Adolescent Relationships

Love
The Joy of Love
The Need of Love
The Cost of Love
How to Love
The Kinds of Love

Suffering
Enduring Suffering
Understanding Suffering
Causes of Suffering
Biblical Suffering
Result of Suffering

Growth
Obstacles to Growth
Steps to Growth
Benefits of Growth
Problems with Growth
Finding Courage for Growth

Beliefs
Unfounded Beliefs
Integrated Beliefs
Beliefs and Behavior
Changing Beliefs
Basic Beliefs

Bible Study
Benefits of Bible Study
Tools of Bible Study
History of Bible Study
How to Study the Bible
Problems of Bible Study

Write your previously chosen subject here _____

What aspect of that subject will you choose as a central theme?

REVIEW

After the following short review, use the space provided to write down a subject and central theme for the talk you will prepare using the SCORRE method. Take time to do this before you move on to the next chapter. The examples of central themes on page 28 may help you. Remember, the central theme will not necessarily express the objective of your talk. It will however represent what you are planning to talk about.

1. There are four basic guidelines to choosing a subject. The first is that the subject must touch the audience. It should meet a specific _____ of the audience or be of _____.

2. The subject must be within the bounds of your _____.

3. The subject may be limited by _____.

4. When speaking on a portion of Scripture the subject should be determined from the _____.

5. Narrowing your focus to a central theme keeps you from trying to cover _____ _____.

6. The subject and central theme may not necessarily express the objective of your talk, but it will represent what you plan to _____ _____.

Answers: 1. *need, interest* 2. *knowledge* 3. *assignment* 4. *text* 5. *too much* 6. *talk about*

Now choose a subject and central theme. Do not be discouraged if you have difficulty narrowing your subject to a central theme. Although the process is not always easy, you will see the fruit of your efforts in clear and powerful presentations. Be brief and clear.

The subject for my talk is _____.

The one aspect of that subject that I am choosing as a central theme is _____.

Chapter Three

THE SCORRE PROCESS—FOCUSING ON THE OBJECTIVE

I have a conviction that no sermon is ready for preaching, not ready for writing out, until we can express its theme in a short, pregnant sentence as clear as crystal. I find the getting of that sentence is the hardest, the most exacting, and the most fruitful labor in my study.

—John Henry Jowett in his
Yale lectures on preaching

This is it! This is the final expression of that pinpoint of focus. It's where the rubber meets the road, where the buck finally stops. As Jowett says, it is the most important aspect of preparing a speech.

Often students ask how preparing a five-minute speech applies to the real world where they must speak for twenty or thirty minutes. My response is, "If you can't say it in five minutes, you won't be able to say it in thirty."

I would go even further and agree with Mr. Jowett. If you can't express the objective of your talk in a single sentence you are not yet focused enough to deliver it in any amount of time. It is the process of writing this sentence that forces you to a powerful focused objective. How to write that sentence will be the objective of this chapter.

WRITING THE OBJECTIVE SENTENCE

The third step in preparing a speech is to write a sentence that embodies the objective of your talk. The objective sentence contains a *proposition*, an *interrogative response*, and a *key word*. This sentence identifies the purpose of your talk and indicates how you will accomplish that purpose. Although it can take several forms it will always look something like this.

> Every person can learn to pray by following the DIRECTIONS given by Christ.

Notice that the sentence contains a *proposition* ("Every person can learn how to pray,") and an *interrogative response* ("by following the DIRECTIONS given by Christ").

An *interrogative response* is an answer to a question. This particular interrogative response answers the question implicit in the proposition: How can every person learn to pray? It also contains a key word. In this sentence the key word is *directions*. Each of the points of this talk should be a direction given by Christ that will help the listener learn how to pray.

Let's look at the steps necessary to write such a sentence. The objective sentence is not just any old sentence pulled from thin air that you think might express the purpose of your talk. You should construct it carefully step by step to force you into a single focus so you can then present the material leading to that focus in an organized and logical fashion.

The sentence may not always be grammatically pretty and rarely will you present it to the audience in that form, but that exact form is necessary as you prepare. It will keep you on track and enable you to discover the single focus for your talk. If you are willing to take the time to put the essence of your talk in this form, you will know exactly what you want to say and how you want to say it. It is only with that kind of confident clarity that you can be assured that the *audience* will grasp what it is you are trying to say.

You may think that insisting on such a focused objective will limit you as a speaker. It may limit the amount of material you can cover, but it will only enhance the power of your message.

One of my students raised an objection: "Not all speeches need an objective. Sometimes a speech is given only to disseminate information."

At this point I asked the student, "Why would the speaker want to give this information?"

There was a long silence as the student realized he was trapped. If he answered my question he would be stating the purpose or objective of the speech. On the other hand if there was no purpose or objective for giving the information then why waste time giving it?

Informational talks are often the most boring. Often it's because the audience rarely understands why the information is important to them.

One of the reasons so many Christians are theologically illiterate is that they have never made the connection between the concepts of theology and the foundation of their faith. That lack of understanding can be traced directly to speakers who give out important information but never take the time to articulate why it is important to their listeners.

HAVING AN OBJECTIVE IS ESSENTIAL TO GOOD COMMUNICATION.

Don't skip lightly over this material. Please take the time to discover the power this kind of focus can bring to your talks.

The actual steps involved in developing an objective sentence are as follows:

1. Write a proposition.

2. Interrogate the proposition with *How?* or *Why?*

3. Write a response to the interrogation.

4. Choose a key word.

Let's look at each of those steps in detail.

Note! Every word in the objective sentence is designed to keep you on track and focused on a single objective. Use the exact words indicated in the examples as you prepare your own speech. Remember, these are not necessarily the exact words you will use when you deliver the speech, but they will help you organize your speech properly.

WRITE A PROPOSITION

In the context of this book, a proposition is a proposal put forth for consideration or acceptance. It will comprise the first half of your objective sentence. The proposition identifies the objective of your speech and provides a powerful focus for the ingredients of your message. Whereas the subject and central theme express *what* you want to talk about, the proposition identifies *why*.

There are three kinds of propositions to choose from. Any speech will fit one of the three. The one you choose will determine the direction of your speech.

The *obligatory* proposition

The *enabling* proposition

The *value* proposition

The Obligatory Proposition

If you are attempting to persuade people with your speech, to motivate the audience to a particular action or view, you have an *obligatory* proposition.

The exact form for writing an obligatory proposition is "Every _____ should _____."

Notice that the obligatory proposition always uses the word should.

The first blank in the sentence is designed to help you identify your target audience. If the message is for teenagers, put the word *teenager* in the blank. If the message is directed to believers, put the word *believer* in the blank. If you are speaking to a general audience, use the word *person*.

The second blank is designed to help you express the actual proposition. Written below are some examples of obligatory propositions, including ones developed from the subjects and central themes discussed in the previous chapter.

> Every *person* should *try horseback riding*.
>
> Every *person* should *consider the sport of skindiving*.
>
> Every *Christian* should *love his or her neighbor*.
>
> Every *speaker* should *pinpoint his or her objective*.

The Enabling Proposition

Informational or instructional speeches often have *enabling* propositions.

The exact form for writing an enabling proposition is "Every _____ can _____."

The enabling proposition always uses the word *can*. The blanks work the same way as in an obligatory speech, but notice the different direction that an enabling speech will take with the same subjects used previously.

Every person can learn to ride a horse.

Every person can learn to skindive.

Every Christian can love his or her neighbor.

Every speaker can learn how to pinpoint his or her objective.

In an *obligatory* speech the speaker tries to convince the audience to take action. In an *enabling* speech the speaker gives instruction or information. Chapter 1 of this book was obligatory in nature. It gave all the reasons why you *should* speak with focus. This chapter has an enabling focus. It shows you *how* you can prepare more focused speeches.

There is a real temptation to include both enabling and obligatory objectives in the same speech, but each message should have only one focused objective. The argument for more than one objective is based on the desire not to leave an audience hanging. If you use an obligatory speech to convince the audience of reasons why they need Christ (obligatory), aren't you obligated to show them *how* to receive him (enabling)? Yes, but not with a speech that contains a dual proposition. In the chapter on putting it all together I will resolve this dilemma. For now, when you write the proposition for your message, be sure to choose only one focus, obligatory or enabling.

The Value Proposition

The *value* proposition is less common. It is used to compare the value of two options and by its structure suggests that one is better than the other. The value proposition requires a great deal of skill to present properly. It also requires a thorough knowledge of the two options that are being compared.

The exact form for writing a value proposition is

"_____ is/are better than _____."

Here are some examples of value propositions.

Dogs are better than *cats.*

Giving is better than *receiving.*

Horseback riding is better than *walking.*

Skindiving is better than *snorkeling.*

Very few speeches lend themselves well to this format, but the ones that do can be very powerful. Be careful not to use this proposition to express what would be better expressed as an obligatory proposition. For example it would not be wise to use the value proposition like this.

Focused speaking is better than *unfocused speaking.*

That would be like saying having a dog is better than not having a dog. Both propositions are more powerful as obligatory propositions:

Every *person* should *speak with focus.*

Every *person* should *own a dog.*

Save value propositions for genuine comparisons that show the benefits of one option over another. For our purposes of learning the basics of the SCORRE system, choose either the obligatory or enabling proposition as you work through your first speech.

How do you decide which proposition to use to present your ideas?

The best way is to write one and see how it fits, bearing in mind that different propositions lead to different speeches on the same theme. For example let's assume that you want to encourage your audience to study the Bible because you know it will help them in their Christian life. Either of the following propositions would work.

> Every *person* can *study the Bible.*

> Every *person* should *study the Bible.*

If you use the enabling proposition, it will lead to a speech on *how* to study the Bible. If, on the other hand, you want to encourage the audience to study the Bible, you should use the obligatory proposition. It will lead to a talk that gives them the reasons *why* they should study. Such a speech would probably list the benefits such a study will bring to their Christian life.

When it comes time to write your proposition it is important to avoid two temptations that can short-circuit your effort. First, avoid the temptation to use the best line from your speech for your proposition. Remember that what you want to say in your speech may be different than what you want to *accomplish* with what you say. Save that burning statement; it will fit in later either in the response to the proposition or in the rationale.

A young pastor preparing a message for an upcoming wedding wrote this as his proposition:

> Every *married couple* should *avoid the pitfalls of marriage.*

He had just read a very helpful book that spoke of these pitfalls and wanted to pass this information on to the couple he was going to marry. However, once he had written the proposition, he was stuck. He had mistaken something he wanted to say in his message with the purpose for his message. After a short discussion it became obvious that he didn't want to deliver a message on the pitfalls of marriage. Instead he wanted to deliver a much more helpful message that would include some information about pitfalls.

I asked him one question that broke the logjam of confusion and helped him see his objective. "Why do you want this young couple to know about the pitfalls of marriage?" I asked.

Without hesitation he responded, "Because I want them to have a successful marriage."

His eyes lit up as he realized he had just stated his real objective. He wanted to help Bill and Mary have a successful marriage. It also was obvious from the beginning that his message was going to be broader than just a discussion of the pitfalls of marriage. He had several guidelines he wanted to share with them. Avoiding the pitfalls of marriage was only one of those guidelines. But because it was burning in his heart, it had found its way to the proposition where it didn't belong.

His final outline looked like this.

> Every *couple* (Bill and Mary) can *increase their chances of having a successful marriage*.

How? (By following three simple guidelines.)

1. Allow Christ to be the head of your home.

2. Follow the advice of Scripture for loving each other.

3. Avoid the pitfalls that destroy marriage.

You will also be tempted to avoid the use of *should* or *can* or otherwise to change the basic structure of the sentence. This is usually a sign that you are trying to include the entire contents of the sermon or speech in the proposition. Remember the proposition expresses the purpose of the message, not its content.

Using one of the forms below, write a proposition that expresses the objective of your talk. Remember this is not in cement. You may come back and change this to express more accurately what you want to accomplish.

My Subject: _____

My Central Theme: _____

My Proposition: _____

Every _____ can _____.

Every _____ should _____.

INTERROGATE THE PROPOSITION

The different types of propositions have different kinds of questions implicit in them. Once you have chosen the kind of proposition you want to use, the next step is to determine what the implicit question is. I call that "interrogating the proposition." The answer to that question will then be the second half of your objective sentence: the interrogatory response.

Obligatory propositions always lead to the question *why*? Enabling propositions lead to the question *how*? Value propositions, like obligatory propositions, lead to the question *why*?

Interrogate your propositions out loud. The answer to the question why or how should lead to the content of your speech. If you are left with a blank and don't know how to answer, then you probably have the wrong proposition.

The young pastor who was preparing to preach at the wedding knew in his heart that he wanted to give his friends guidelines that would help them in their marriage. Yet when he wrote the wrong proposition it did not lead him to the message that was brewing in his heart:

> Every couple should avoid the pitfalls of marriage.

Why? This led nowhere. You avoid pitfalls because they are pitfalls.

However, when he correctly identified his proposition and then interrogated it with the correct question *(How?)*, he could hardly stop talking.

Many times it is easier to identify what we want to talk about than it is to identify the purpose of the talk. That is why writing a clear proposition is so important.

Here are some examples of different propositions developed from the same subject. Match the potential messages on the right with the proposition on the left that will most likely fit that message.

Possible propositions	Potential messages
1. Obligatory Every person should practice biblical love. Why?	a. A message that compares atheism with belief in God.
2. Enabling Every person can practice biblical love. How?	b. A message detailing the benefits of practicing biblical love.
3. Value *Agape* love is better than *eros* love. Why?	c. A message that gives three steps that show how to deal with conflict.
4. Obligatory Every person should believe in God.	d. A message that compares two different kinds of love.
5. Enabling Every person can believe in God with confidence.	e. A message that gives four reasons we can believe with confidence.
6. Value Theism is better than atheism.	f. A message that details the consequences of not facing conflict.
7. Obligatory Every person should learn to deal with conflict.	g. A message that instructs how to love as God commanded in Scripture.
8. Enabling Every person can learn to deal with conflict.	h. A message that answers the question "Why should I believe?"

If the above information has motivated you to change the wording of your proposition, rewrite your proposition here. Keep in mind that as you develop the entire objective you may want to make further changes.

Every _____ should/can _____.

WRITING AN INTERROGATIVE RESPONSE

Once you have interrogated your proposition with *how* or *why*, it's time to answer the question and write the second half of the sentence, the interrogative response. This response is a prepositional phrase containing a key word. To keep you focused you should write the propositional phrase in a specific form.

The response to an *obligatory* proposition should always begin with the words *because of.*

> Every *person* should *love his or her neighbor* because of *the COMMANDS given in Scripture.*

> Every *person* should *learn to ride a horse* because of *the unique QUALITIES of the sport.*

There are times when you will be tempted to substitute the word *for* in place of *because of* because it sounds better. Don't give in to this temptation. *Because of* will keep you focused. Substitutions lead to sloppiness and confusion. Remember this is an exercise to help you pinpoint your objective. You don't have to use the same wording when you deliver your message.

The response to an *enabling* proposition should always begin with the word *by.*

Every Christian can learn to love his or her neighbor by following the INSTRUCTIONS of Christ.

Every person can learn to ride a horse by taking three easy STEPS.

The response to *value* propositions should always begin with the words *because of.*

Dogs are better than cats because of three genetic TRAITS.

CHOOSING A KEY WORD

Notice that I have put one word in each of the above responses in capital letters and that in each case the word is a plural noun. Those are the key words. The key word is one of the most important words in your objective sentence. It is always a plural noun, and it should lead beyond itself, opening up the possibilities of the talk.

Without a key word the objective degenerates into a statement rather than a proposition. Consider this objective:

Every person can learn to pray by reading the Bible.

Notice that there is no plural noun. As a result this sentence becomes a simple statement of fact. There is no message to preach. The sentence does not lead the audience to want more information.

Now look at the following objective:

Every person can learn to pray by taking two simple steps.

The key word is *steps* and it causes the audience to ask, "What steps?" Undoubtedly one of the steps will be to follow the example Christ gave in the Bible. Another might be to practice by praying daily.

Suppose that the speaker wanted all of his message to come from the biblical instructions given for prayer. Then his objective sentence would read as follows:

> Every person can learn to pray by following the instructions given in the Bible.

The key word *instructions* causes the audience to ask, "What instructions?"

Always include a key word!

Three rules should govern your choice of this word.

1. It must be a plural noun.

2. It should be as memorable as possible.

3. It must be a word that describes all the rationale (points) of your speech.

A corollary to the second rule is that you should avoid using nondescript words like *ways*, *things*, or *stuff* as key words. Communicator Jim Green told me he had an English teacher who would fail any paper that contained the word *things*. She explained, "If you tell me to go up on the mountain where there are trees and things, I will refuse to budge until I find out what 'things' are." She is right. Those things could be innocent rocks or a band of murdering alien beings. The reader or listener will never know, unless you tell what the things are.

Although there is a proper time to use the word *things*, most of the time we use it because we are too lazy to think of the more proper, more powerful key word. Look at the list of sample key words on pages 44-47. Any one of them could be replaced with the word *things*, but their color and beauty would be lost in the process.

The key word is like a bag that holds the logical rationale of your speech. Each of your rationale will be derivatives of the key word. For instance if your key word is *commands*, then each of the points of your speech will be a command.

Consider the following objective sentence:

> Every person should try skindiving because of the THRILLS associated with this sport.

Every point in your speech will detail one of the thrills associated with the sport of skindiving.

Or consider this objective sentence for a sermon:

> Every Christian can test the will of God by taking the ACTIONS Paul suggests in Romans 12:1–2.

Every point in this sermon will be one of the actions that Paul suggests in that portion of Scripture.

A properly chosen key word will make your speech more focused, easier to understand, and easier to remember. It will keep your speech right on track.

Resource Sheet
Examples of Key Words*

abuses	beliefs	comparisons
actualities	benefits	conceptions
accusations	blemishes	concessions
affairs	blessings	corrections
affirmations	blockades	criteria
agreements	blots	criticisms
alternatives	blows	crowns
angles	blunders	cults
answers	boasts	cultures
applications	bonds	customs
approaches	books	dangers
areas	boundaries	debts
arguments	breaches	decisions
aspects	burdens	declarations
aspirations	calls	deeds
assertions	categories	deficiencies
assumptions	causes	definitions
assurances	certainties	degrees
attitudes	challenges	departments
attributes	changes	details
axioms	charges	differences
barriers	circumstances	directives
beginnings	commands	disciplines

---

* Adapted from *Manual for Biblical Preaching* by Lloyd Perry (Grand Rapids: Baker, n.d.), 68.

disclosures
discoveries
divisions
doctrines
doors
doubts
dreams
duties
editions
effects
elements
encouragements
examples
excesses
exchanges
exclamations
experiments
explanations
exponents
exposures
expressions
extremes
facets
factors
facts
faculties
failures
falls
families
faults

fears
feelings
fields
finalities
flaws
forces
formalities
forms
foundations
functions
fundamentals
gains
generalizations
gifts
graces
groups
guarantees
guides
habits
handicaps
honors
hopes
hungers
hurts
ideals
ideas
idols
ills
imitations
impacts

imperatives
imperfections
implements
implications
impossibilities
impressions
improvements
inadequacies
incentives
incidents
invitations
irritations
issues
items
joys
judgments
justifications
keys
kinds
labors
lapses
laws
lessons
levels
liabilities
liberties
lights
limits
links
lists

loads

locations

looks

losses

loyalties

manners

marks

materials

means

measures

meetings

members

memories

mercies

methods

ministries

misfortunes

mistakes

models

moods

motives

mountains

movements

mysteries

names

narratives

natures

necessities

needs

nights

norms

notes

numbers

objectives

objects

obligations

observances

observations

obstacles

occasions

occurrences

offenses

offer

offices

omissions

operations

opinions

opponents

options

orders

organizations

origins

panaceas

parables

paradoxes

paragraphs

parallels

particulars

parties

parts

paths

patterns

peaks

peculiarities

penalties

perceptions

perfections

performances

perils

periods

perplexities

personalities

persons

petitions

phases

philosophies

phrases

pictures

pieces

places

plagues

plans

pleas

pledges

plots

points

positions

possibilities	qualities	sacrifices
powers	quantities	satisfactions
practices	queries	sayings
prayers	questions	scales
precautions	quests	scars
predicaments	quotas	schemes
predictions	quotations	schools
premises	ranks	seals
preparations	ratings	seasons
prescriptions	reactions	secrets
pressures	reasons	selections
pretensions	recommendations	sentiments
principles	records	sequences
privileges	recruits	services
prizes	references	shields
problems	regions	situations
processes	regulations	skills
products	rejections	solicitations
profits	relapses	solutions
prohibitions	relations	sources
promises	responses	spheres
proofs	restraints	statements
prophecies	results	states
propositions	revelations	steps
prospects	rewards	stipulations
provisions	roads	stresses
punishments	roles	strokes
purposes	roots	styles
pursuits	routes	subjects
qualifications	rules	sufferings

superiorities
superlatives
supports
suppositions
symptoms
systems
tactics
talents
tasks
teachings
tendencies
tests
theories
theses
thoughts
ties
times
titles
tokens
tones
topics
traces
trials
triumphs
troubles
truths
types
uncertainties
undertakings
units

urges
uses
vacancies
values
variations
varieties
ventures
verifications
views
violations
virtues
visions
vocations
voices
wants
warnings
ways
weaknesses
weapons
words
works
worries
wrongs
yokes
zones

Once you have constructed a sentence following the four steps above, that sentence is your objective. Coming up with that sentence will be the most difficult and most important part of any message. If you wish to try to write an objective sentence using the subject and central theme you developed earlier, use the four steps to do so now. However, do not be discouraged if you find it difficult or seem to run into a brick wall. Eventually, you will begin to see how it all fits together. You may find it helpful to read the next chapter on *rationale* and then come back to work on your objective sentence.

My Subject: _____

My Central Theme: _____

(from pp. 25ff.)

My Proposition from page _____

Obligatory objective:

Every _____ should _____

because of _____.

Enabling objective:

Every _____ can _____

by _____.

Identify the plural noun in each objective that functions as a key word and circle it.

REVIEW

Review the items below. You need to understand all of them to write a clear and focused objective.

1. What are the three kinds of propositions?

   a. _____ b. _____ c. _____

2. What are the four steps to writing an objective sentence?

   Step 1: Write a _____.

   Step 2: _____ the proposition with *how* or *why*.

   Step 3: Write a _____ to the interrogation.

   Step 4: Choose a _____ word.

3. Obligatory propositions are always interrogated with _____.

4. Enabling propositions are always interrogated with _____.

5. Value propositions are always interrogated with _____.

6. The interrogative response is a prepositional phrase containing a _____ word.

7. The response to an obligatory proposition should always begin with the words _____ _____.

8. The response to an enabling proposition should always begin with the word _____.

9. The response to a value proposition should always begin with the words _____ _____.

10. The key word is always a plural _____ .

11. When you have constructed a sentence that contains a proposition, an interrogative response, and a key word, that sentence is your _____ .

Answers: 1. a. *obligatory* b. *enabling* c. *value* 2. Step 1: *proposition* Step 2: *interrogate* Step 3: *response* Step 4: *key* 3. *why* 4. *how* 5. *why* 6. *key* 7. *because of* 8. *by* 9. *because of* 10. *noun* 11. *objective*

Chapter Four

SPEAKING WITHIN REASON— DEVELOPING THE RATIONALE AND EVALUATING THE SPEECH

In the SCORRE process everything narrows until you have written your objective, the pinpointed focus that you have worked so hard to achieve. Then the process reverses itself, broadening to build a solid base of information to support your objective. The first step in that broadening process is to build organized and convincing rationale.

The *rationale*, more commonly known as the main points of the speech, establishes a logical foundation upon which the credibility of your speech will rest. If the *key word* is the bag that will hold all the elements of the talk, then the *rationale* is the contents of the bag.

There are three rules that will govern your choice of rationale.

1. The rationale must correspond to the key word.

Consider using the following objective statement for your speech:

> Every Christian should love his or her neighbor because of the COMMANDS given in Scripture.

Each of the points of your speech (the rationale) must be a command that is given in Scripture. You can see how this will keep all the elements of your talk related to the proposition. Everything you say will be the explanation or exposition of a command in Scripture that encourages the believer to love his or her neighbor.

If you wanted to broaden the scope of rationale you could use *reasons* as a key word:

> Every Christian should love his or her neighbor because of three REASONS.

With *reasons* as a key word, one of the reasons might be "the commands given in Scripture," but you would not be limited to commands.

This rationale could also be narrowed in focus by changing the phrase that modifies the key word.

For example, you could use the following objective:

> Every person should love his or her neighbor because of the COMMANDS given by Christ in Scripture.

Now each part of your rationale will be more than just a command or even a command given in Scripture. Each part must be a command found in Scripture that was given by Christ himself.

Even a single adjective will affect the rationale you choose. Each of the following objective sentences contains the same proposition and key word, but the different adjectives will subtly change the rationale and, as a result, the direction of the speech.

> Every person should go skindiving because of three health BENEFITS.

Every person should go skindiving because of three environmental BENEFITS.

Every person should go skindiving because of three educational BENEFITS.

Benefits is still the key word. Each part of the rationale must not only be a benefit, but it must be the kind of benefit indicated by the adjective.

2. **The rationale should be stated as briefly as possible.**

There is a real tendency to try to include all the information in a sermon or speech in the rationale. It is much more important that the rationale be short and memorable. The rationale should serve as a sharp memory hook upon which the contents of your speech will hang.

3. **Parts of the rationale should be parallel in grammatical form.**

If the rational is the logic that will lead the audience to the objective, then it important that it be stated in a form that is easy to remember. Assume that the key word is *facts* then look at the following rational.

FACT #1. It is rare

FACT #2. It is valuable

FACT #3. Handle it carefully

The third part breaks two of the rules above. First, it is not stated as a fact. "Handle it carefully" may be an instruction, a direction, or a command, but it's not a fact. Second, it is not written in the same grammatical form as the other two. This can be solved by changing the wording to "it is fragile."

The person who wrote this rationale wanted to caution his listeners to handle the merchandise carefully. He gave in to the temptation to put that statement in his rationale. Under the heading *It is fragile*, he can still give the instruction to handle it carefully and keep the main points of his speech memorable.

At first glance this rule may seem trivial, but there is good reason for it. The human mind looks for patterns and hooks to help with comprehension and memory. A similar grammatical pattern provides such a hook. If I gave a talk on three facts you should know about handling antique china, and if I stated my rationale as originally listed above, you would have difficulty remembering the third part because it wouldn't fit with the others.

Your rationale will not always fit into neat three-word sentences, but every effort you make to keep them short and parallel in form will be worth it. It is unreasonable to expect that the audience will remember the entire speech. But if your rationale is clear and memorable, people will remember the basics of your talk long after you have made your exit.

Remember that during the whole process of SCORRE you are looking for the best combination of ingredients to make your speech focused and clear. As you prepare the rationale for a speech you might discover that the rationale you want to use doesn't fit your previously chosen key word. Simply go back and choose a more appropriate key word to describe the rationale.

For example, you might decide that the following rationale best fits your talk on handling precious china.

Research its history

Know its value

Handle it carefully

Your key word in this case should be *steps* or *directions* or any other key word that is most descriptive.

When you have finally written your objective sentence and identified your rationale you have the most basic outline necessary for any speech. Once you have learned the process you can experiment with how you are most comfortable coming to this point.

For example, when I am preparing a talk, I write my objective sentence first. Then, as I define my rationale to my satisfaction I go back and make sure I have chosen the most powerful key word to describe my rationale.

Expository preachers almost always look for the rationale listed in the text and then study the context for the intent of the author. At other times the objective of the author is clearly stated, and only a close study of the broader context of Scripture reveals the rationale for such an objective.

No matter which process you choose, the final result should fit together and focus on that single objective you wish to achieve. The SCORRE process is designed to help you focus on a single objective and decide what material you will use to support that objective.

When you have written your objective sentence and rationale the next step is to add flesh to the basic outline. Now is the time to add the illustrations, data, anecdotes, and humor—the *resources*—that will bring the talk to life.

As you choose which resources you are going to use keep these facts in mind.

1. Resources should bring light and color to your talk.

My hometown of Denver has a wonderful piece of architecture called the City and County Building. For 335 days out of the year, hundreds and thousands of people drive by this stately building with its Roman columns and never give it a glance. All that changes in the Christmas season. During that time of the year the city spends thousands of dollars lighting the structure with colored flood lights. People come from all over to see this beautiful sight. The building doesn't change but the lights cause a new appreciation for what was there all along. The lights by themselves would draw little attention, but when they are focused on the building, they make people notice what was ignored before.

Resources work the same way in a talk. God's expression of love through the suffering of Christ may seem like a distant, unmoving story until an illustration of an earthly father faced with the same sacrifice snaps it into the clear focus of reality.

2. Resources should make the audience want to listen.

The human mind is capable of miraculous feats, but it is hard-pressed to concentrate for any extended period of time. An endless stream of information without the color of illustrations will leave your audience looking out the window and thinking about their income tax return or the

roast cooking in the oven. The mind will tend to wander unless it is held by illustrations, humor, or supportive resources.

3. Resources should clarify and strengthen your rationale.

Sometimes the audience may question your rationale, and you may need to prove your points. In situations like this your resources can provide the evidence to prove the statement you have made.

Suppose you are encouraging the youth in your class to share Christ with their friends. One of the reasons (key word) you give is that their friends are living lives of quiet desperation. Very few teenagers would accept that statement at face value. Yet when they hear you say that suicide is the second greatest killer of teenagers, they will find it more credible. If you can further support your rationale with illustrations or the testimony of a peer that help them to identify their own desperation, they will be ready to believe that what you say is true.

4. Resources should never be an end in themselves.

Just because you've heard a great story or powerful illustration is not reason enough to include it in your talk. Many times I have observed a speaker use up fifteen minutes of a twenty-minute talk telling a story that only marginally supported some minute point. (Many times I was that speaker.) When that happens the real focus of the talk gets lost.

As one who uses humor extensively I often think of new illustrations even as I talk. There was a time I would include such a story or illustration just because it was funny and would make people laugh. But this is disruptive to clear communication.

Some speakers develop their entire talk around an interesting illustration rather than any specific objective. In this case, they are working with an unstated, perhaps even unconscious, objective:

> I must structure the evening so I can tell this one entertaining story.

As entertainment it might work, but when it comes to communication the result is disastrous. Never let the resources become an end in themselves.

The chapter on illustrations goes deeper into the process of finding, filing, and retrieving good illustrations. The next section was designed to help you understand how resources should fit into the SCORRE process.

EVALUATION

The process of evaluation should be one that continues throughout the preparation and delivery of a message. You should ask yourself the following questions repeatedly as you prepare. They will also serve as a review of the material covered in this chapter.

Do my subject, central theme, objective sentence, and rationale all fit together in an organized and logical manner?

Do I have the right proposition?

Have I interrogated my proposition properly?

Is my response written properly, with clarity, and does it contain the best key word?

Do the parts of my rationale match the key word, and are they brief and clear?

How can I give my audience a way to respond to what they will hear?

Does the message I am preparing touch the listeners at some point of need in their life?

Do I know what I am talking about?

Do I have enough information to speak with intelligence on the subject or Scripture I have chosen?

Is my life consistent with the truth I am presenting?

Is what I am presenting true to the Scripture under consideration?

Am I excited about fleshing out this message and presenting it?

Continue to evaluate even the most carefully prepared message right up until its presentation. If the youth leader who plowed through the regular lesson after the death of two students in his group had stopped to evaluate, he probably would have responded differently. Surely he would have realized that his audience would come to church with a deep hurt and he would have been prepared to respond to that need.

With small informal groups, you may find yourself making adjustments as you speak. One night I was in the middle of presenting a carefully prepared message on loneliness when one of the youth in my group interrupted. "What I want to know," she shouted, "is how can I know Jesus personally."

"We cover that in two weeks," I snapped, a little upset that she would be rude enough to interrupt my carefully prepared talk.

I bulldozed my way through another point only to have another student interrupt. "What good is it for us to deal with loneliness until we know how to accept Jesus for ourselves?"

Suddenly the realization hit me. This audience was not willing to wait two weeks to hear how they could trust Christ. They wanted to know right then. How could I lay aside the notes I had spent hours preparing? The answer was simple. I *had* to lay them aside. My group was hungry for something else that night. With a prayer for God's help I put my speech aside and presented the simple plan of salvation. That night twelve students responded to the grace offered by Christ. I had prepared my message blind to the needs of my audience. It took the bold interruption of a fifteen-year-old girl to cause me to reevaluate.

It probably won't happen to you often, but be aware that on rare occasions the Holy Spirit may ask you to make the final evaluation of your message even as you are giving it.

Most last-minute evaluations affect the tone of your message, not its structure. You may have planned to deliver your message with a tone of exhortation, but that tone may not be right for the temperament of the audience. A good helping of love and understanding may drive your message deeper than the authoritative lecture you had planned to give. Similarly, the humorous tone you planned for a speech may not be appropriate for an audience that has just gone through difficult circumstances.

When presenting the gospel, every word of your presentation is important. It is a message that can lead the listener from death to life. If I am going to talk to you about the thrills of skindiving, I want to keep you interested, informed, and entertained. If I am going to talk to you about the love of Christ, I will evaluate ten times as hard because I want to do more than keep your interest or to entertain. The vital importance of that message demands that I communicate. As you prepare and as you speak, evaluate every step of the way

Chapter Five

FINDING, FILING, AND RETRIEVING ILLUSTRATIONS

One of the elements that characterizes the effective communicator is the use of timely, powerful illustrations. A good illustration has the power to lift what appears to be an abstract idea to a position of interest and practical application. It can snap a wandering mind back to attention, convince a doubting mind of truth, and clarify a difficult concept.

You can enhance the dynamics of your communication by adopting the practices presented in this chapter for finding, filing, and retrieving good illustrations.

Before you can use illustrations, you have to find them. This turns out to be easier than it sounds. The best illustrations are all around you. You can begin by starting to notice them. Then you can supplement the real-life experiences you encounter with other valuable resources for illustrations. And finally, the trick is to develop a filing system that helps you find these illustrations when you need to use them.

CAPTURING LIFE'S ILLUSTRATIONS

If you wish to capture good illustrations, you will have to develop two expert skills: the eye of the hunter and the pencil of the gunfighter.

Look

You need the eye of the hunter to recognize good illustrations when you see them. Most of us go through life with a kind of tunnel vision that causes us to pass up hundreds of potentially good illustrations every day. Every time you go for a walk, read a book, listen to a speaker, or go to the supermarket, you are in prime hunting territory to gather excellent illustrations. Yet you will pass hundreds without being aware of them unless you develop the eye of the hunter.

When I first started driving to Estes Park, Colorado, with the Dynamic Communicators staff, we passed through some of the finest big game country in the world. Because I have hunted all my life I have trained myself to be on the lookout for game at all times. Often I would spot elk or deer standing in the forest near the road and without thinking would jam on the brakes. The car would screech to a halt instantly, and then I would spend the next fifteen minutes trying to get my passengers to see what I had trained my eyes to see. "See the big rock about half way up the mountain?" I would whisper, pointing frantically in the direction of the animal that seemed so obvious. "Look just to the left of that big rock, under the tallest pine tree." Sometimes after physically holding their heads in the direction of the animal and sighting down the part in their hair I could get my friends to see what I saw. Occasionally the animal would wander off before they could spot it. After several years I have taught my friends to have the eye of a hunter. Now they know what to look for and often spot animals before I do.

Animals, like illustrations, seldom stand out in the open so you can see them from head to tail. They are partially obscured by trees, bushes, and other vegetation. The hunter develops a sharp eye for the clues that will alert him to the presence of an animal. For example, horizontal lines are a clue. They are present in the forest in only two basic forms. The back of a large animal such as a deer and the line formed by a fallen tree. If you see a horizontal line seventy feet long it's not likely to be a deer. However, if you see a short horizontal line with legs, you can be fairly sure it's not a tree.

The color white is another clue. In the summer, the color white is seldom found in Colorado forests except on the rump of an animal. Close investigation of a small patch of white will often reveal the partially hidden body of an elk or deer. Any patch of white is worth investigating.

Black buttons are another clue. In the winter rabbits turn white and are perfectly camouflaged against the snow. But their eyes don't turn white. Many times I have stared for long minutes at a round black button in the brush only a few feet from where I stood. I couldn't see a rabbit, only the button. As I stepped forward for a closer look the button would bound away, now connected to the totally visible body of a snowshoe hare.

The illustrations that we encounter in everyday life are like those animals hidden in the forest. They are partially hidden by our preoccupation and the circumstances that surround them. We don't think of them as good illustrations because they don't seem dramatic enough. Yet it is this very camouflaging connection with everyday life that makes them real and powerful.

Once when I was working on a speech on teenagers who fall away from the faith when they leave home, I almost missed a powerful illustration.

I was on an airplane, and a small child was running up and down the aisles. Although she was a beautiful child, her unsupervised shenanigans were disturbing several passengers. This all came to an abrupt halt when she crawled over an empty seat and fell into the lap of a business man behind her, putting a bruise on his head in the process.

The angry business man called a flight attendant who quickly brought the child to her mother and instructed her to keep her in her seat. The mother set the little girl down, pulled the seat belt tight across her lap and ordered, "Now you sit still." The girl sat absolutely still, but she had a huge, mischievous grin on her face.

"Why are you smiling," the mother snapped.

"Because," the little girl smirked, "I may be sitting on the outside, but on the inside I'm still running around."

I almost let it pass as a simple snide remark from an undisciplined and unruly child, and then I saw the rest of the animal hidden in the brush. This was a perfect illustration of one of the points I was considering in my speech. Many times we restrain the outside behavior of teenagers in the church without considering what is on the inside. These

kids remain dutifully obedient as long as the seat belt of rules is enforced. Yet if we do nothing to change their inner attitudes, they'll release the seat belt as soon as they leave home, and the inner person will come out. What may have seemed like genuine faith will have turned out to be only outward restraint.

Over the last several years I have trained myself to look for the telltale clues that indicate there might be an illustration hiding nearby. Discipline yourself to look for the signs. Have the eye of a hunter. Don't allow people and events around you to slip by unnoticed. Become an observer. Just learning to watch people will bring to you a rich source of illustrations that you once passed by without even a glance.

What are the telltale signs to look for? Quite simply it boils down to this: if something catches your attention, if it stirs your emotions, that's a sign that it's a likely candidate for an illustration. If an event in your everyday life has that effect on *you*, chances are good that it will do the same for an audience. Anything out of the ordinary should snap you to full attention. That rude driver who cut you off in traffic (though perhaps that is not out of the ordinary), the little boy who asks a bizarre question, the story in the newspaper of the cat who followed a family after they moved five hundred miles—all these provide excellent possibilities for bringing light and color to the truth in your talks.

But spotting good illustrations does you no good, unless you record them, because you'll never remember them all. That's where wielding a pencil with the skill of a gunfighter comes in.

I have lost count of the times I have seen or heard an excellent illustration and made a mental note to use it sometime. If you are anything like me, a mental note is no note at all. Someone will share a joke that makes me roar with laughter, I make a mental note to share it with my family and forget the whole thing within seconds. I remember that I heard a great story, it's just that I have no idea what the story was. If I were restricted in this chapter to giving you just one idea that would help you use better illustrations, I would say this:

When you hear, see, or read a good illustration, write it down!

Einstein said that he never wasted brain power trying to remember what could be written down. Most of us don't have that much brain power to waste. An old Chinese proverb says, "The faintest ink has a better memory than the sharpest brain." Carry your pencil just as a gun fighter carries a gun. Have a pad and pencil with you at all times. When you observe something that has the potential of a good illustration, your hand should go to your pocket faster than lightning. I'm not kidding about this. On more than one occasion a thought has slipped my mind while I searched my pockets for a pencil. In fact, if you are over forty it might be a good idea to keep the lead of the pencil on the paper at all times.

Write down the details of the illustration and, the instant you are aware of it, how you think it could be used. This is especially true with original thoughts that come to you at unexpected times. Often when listening to other speakers, I find their words will trigger a tangential thought in my mind. Rather than try to juggle that thought and listen to the speaker at the same time, I write it down for later development.

The best ideas come to me just before I go to sleep. You should always keep a pad and pencil by your bed, but be sure that you write your thoughts out in detail.

One night I awoke from a dream that left me in a cold sweat. I knew the dream would make an excellent illustration so I reached over for my pad and pencil. In the dark I wrote my most prominent memory of the dream and fell back to sleep. In the morning I awoke and quickly reached for the pad. Scrawled across the center of the pad was the word chicken. To this day I can remember how frightening the dream was, but I have no idea what the dream was about or what a chicken had to do with it. On another occasion I wrote a detailed account of one of my nighttime originals with the eraser end of the pencil.

Whether you are lying in bed or wide awake sitting in a dentist chair, write the illustration or idea in detail or you will forget it. Some people dictate their thoughts into a small tape recorder they keep with them at all times. That works fine if you have a secretary who will transcribe what you have recorded every day. I found it difficult to search though all of the material on the tape to get to the illustration I wanted. I used to keep the machine by my bed until one night in the dark I dictated a wonderful illustration into the remote control unit for the television. I have no idea what the illustration was, but I know it was a great one and it's in there somewhere.

SUPPLEMENTING YOUR OWN EXPERIENCES WITH QUALITY RESOURCES

Bible

The first and most important of these supplementary resources is the Word of God. Anyone who communicates the gospel should be familiar with it. The Bible is more than a good book of illustrations. It is the source of the very truth that we proclaim. However, the person who is constantly searching the Word of God for direction in life will be able to illustrate the truth in that book far more effectively than one who simply uses it to prepare messages.

A pastor once said, "I do not study that I might preach, but because I study I must preach." As you and I expose ourselves to the Word of God and allow it to direct our lives, we enrich the power of illustrating its truth. The fact that the Bible is more than just a resource for illustrations does not negate the fact that it is a great source of illustrations. But it must be read with the eye of the hunter.

Books

Books are another important resource of illustrations. Being well read is a quality that separates a great communicator from a mediocre one and brings credibility and depth to any presentation. Someone has said that the two things that will have the most profound influence on your life are the people you meet and the books you read. I would not hesitate to claim that those are also the two richest resources for illustrations.

Secrets of Dynamic Communication

Magazines

The Christian communicator should read enough secular and Christian literature to keep abreast of current developments. Magazines such as *Time* or *Newsweek* will keep the speaker informed on what is going on in the world. They are also a rich source of illustrations.

While preparing a message entitled "Victory in Jesus" I came across an article in *Time* about Dan Jansen, the speed skater who fell twice in the 1988 Winter Olympics. His sister had died of cancer just hours before his first race. *Time* recorded the sad drama that ended years of sacrifice and physical preparation.

> It was an anxious and grieving Jansen on the starting line that evening. At the outset he jumped the gun. To avoid a repeat and disqualification, he held back for a crucial moment at the second gun, then bore down to make up for lost time. He went down suddenly in the first turn ... then he fell the second time, on the straightaway of Thursday's 1,000-meter event, just 200 meters short of the finish. It was even more stunning, as if he had been forced down by sorrow alone. Watching from the Gallery, brother Mike, 24, had just assured a sister: "Dan's made it through the toughest turns. He's fine now." At the 600-meter mark, Janzen was .31 seconds faster than any of the competition, then his right skate "caught an edge"— hit the ice on the side instead of the bottom of the blade—sending him to his hands and knees and into a wall. For a moment he sat on the ice, unbelieving, until Coach Mike Crowe and teammate Nick Thometz came over to help him off. Arriving at the

bench area, he embraced his fiancée, Canadian speed
skater Natalie Grenier, and sobbed....

(*Time*, February 29, 1988, p. 87)

Why would this strike me as an illustration for Christian
victory? Because I so identified with that hopeless feeling.
Because I was reading with the eye of the hunter, I was
suddenly aware of the hope we have in Christ. For Dan
Jansen there may not be another chance, but Christ
always extends his hand even in the most hopeless
moments, offering to pick us up and give us a new start.
Christianity Today and *Christian Herald*, among others, give
the speaker a Christian view of current events and both
are filled with excellent quotes and resources. *Youth
Worker Update*, published by Youth Specialties, is a magazine I recommend to those who work with youth. It is
always full of timely material.

Newspapers

Every morning an economical resource for illustrations is
delivered right to your door. A recent newspaper ran two
news items side by side that revealed the tragically
warped values that permeate our society. A story in the
left column applauded the militant efforts of a group
called Animal Rights to ban all hunting and trapping of
fur-bearing animals on the grounds that it was cruel and
violated the animals' rights. On the right side of the page
was an article that openly ridiculed the efforts of the
right-to-life movement to protect unborn babies from
death by abortion. I'm sure this juxtaposition was unin-
tentional, but it served to show the absurd contrast of values. Not only was it obvious animals were considered to

have the same rights as human beings but the immediate opportunity to compare these stories clearly showed that animal life was considered more valuable than human life. It was wrong to take the fur of an animal for the sake of convenience and comfort, but it was okay to take the life of an unborn child for the same reason. Either story by itself was not so powerful as the contrast of seeing them together. Learn to read your newspaper with the eye of a hunter.

Other Sources

Signs and bumper stickers will often provide a resource of illustrations. One of the most poignant bumper stickers I have encountered was "Don't follow me—I'm lost." It was designed to be a funny comment on the condition of travelers, but what a powerful and tragic comment about the condition of those who are without Christ.

Sometimes a quote or casual remark will provide a powerful illustration that drives your point home. I frequently lecture on the importance of humor in everyday life. A remark attributed to Victor Borge provided a perfect highlight for my view of the value of humor. He is reported to have said, "Humor is the shortest distance between two people."

By now nearly everyone has heard of the little girl who misquoted the Twenty-Third Psalm. When asked to recite, she stood with prim confidence and declared, "The Lord is my shepherd and that's all I want."

Keep your ears and eyes sharp for those brief, sharp, fresh quotes. Many pastors who go to conferences with pen and pencil ready as well-known speakers address the crowd never take advantage of the late-night fellowship and hallway conversations that are rich with comments and quotes. Lay speakers and teachers search the lesson guides and illustration books for just the right story only to ignore the wealth of illustrations at work and in their own home.

If you are a public speaker you should be searching with the eyes and ears of a hunter every minute of the day for those gems that will make your talks unforgettable. Those short, powerful quotes can help your audience remember the point of your talk long after they've forgotten the rest.

The powerful encouragement to persevere to the end found in Hebrews 12 was burned into my heart by a quote from Winston Churchill. Speaking at a college graduation, he must have given one of the shortest addresses in history. He walked to the platform and in that commanding voice boomed, "Never give up, never give up, never give up." Then he sat down. Whenever I get discouraged, those words come to my mind, but they do not come alone. They are like an anchor attached to the more important truth in Hebrews 12. They are the lights that bring my attention to the beautiful architecture of that passage, a passage that suggests very specific *actions* that will enable me never to give up.

Careful observation of human behavior will reveal more illustrations than you can possibly use. During a trip to Disneyland I was reminded of how we allow circumstances to affect our expressions of love. As we entered the park I watched a young mother dressed in a bright pink dress escorting her small boy into the park. "Today we are going to see a big duck and a big mouse and go on some fun rides," she bubbled as they faded into the crowd. I spotted her pink dress again at the end of the day as we were leaving the park. It had been about 95 degrees all day, and the park was saturated with sweaty people. The rides required an hour wait in line. After eight hours of waiting in hot lines this tired mother had the same energetic little boy by the same arm. But this time she was jerking him along giving him gruff details about what his father was going to do to him when he got home. I'm sure this mother loved her little boy. But her ability to show it was affected by the temperature and the condition of her feet.

The final resource of illustrations that we often pass up completely is one that many famous speakers and preachers use. It is the resource of network. Many of these popular men and women rely on a steady stream of articles, book excerpts, and observations passed on to them by friends and associates. You may not have the money to hire someone to research illustrations for you, but you do have friends and associates.

About three years ago I started asking my friends to send me cartoons, illustrations, magazine articles, and quotes that struck them as unique and interesting. Those informal requests resulted in a constant source of great illustrations I would never have discovered on my own. A friend gave me the Victor Borge quote on humor. A friend in Youth for Christ delivered the following zinger. "Christianity is a lot like football. There are 22,000 people in the stands who desperately need exercise watching 22 people on the field who desperately need rest." (Did you like that? If so, get that pencil out and write it down.)

One last suggestion. In high school I worked hard to expand my vocabulary beyond the two words *far out*. My teacher encouraged us to use new words in conversation the same day we learned them. To memorize the names of people use the name immediately after hearing it. The same is true of a new illustration. Do more than just write it down. Share it with several friends. Then you will be more prepared to use it with power when you deliver it in your speech.

FILING AND RETRIEVING GOOD ILLUSTRATIONS

If you follow consistently the steps listed previously, you will have more illustrations than you can use. To get the most out of this pool of resources it is important to have some way of filing and retrieving them when you need them. Here are some suggestions on how to do that with each kind of illustration.

First it will be necessary to construct a topical file that will help you retrieve illustrations as you need them. You don't have to make the file exhaustive when you start. It will grow with your collection. You can keep this file either in a computer data base or in a set of file folders in a drawer. If you have a system for cross referencing, your file can be more compact.

The system I will describe is a file folder system. Although it is the most bulky, it is easy to describe. You should be able to modify it easily to work with either of the other systems. Work with what is most comfortable for you. Here is a list of topics to get you started. As illustrations lend themselves to new topics simply add those to your existing files.

Possible Headings for a Topical File

Abuse	Easter	Marriage
Advertising	Ethics	Materialism
Aging	Evangelism	Media
Apologetics	Faith	Missions
Atheism	Family	Money
Bible	Fear	Morality
Boredom	Forgiveness	Movies
Cheating	Freedom	Obedience
Christ	Friends	Obesity
Christmas	God	Parents
Church	Growth	Peer Pressure
Communication	Guilt	Phonies
Competition	Giving	Poverty
Confession	Halloween	Prayer
Conformity	Heaven	Pride
Counseling	Holy Spirit	Problems
Creation	Honesty	Racism
Crucifixion	Hunger	Religion
Cults	Holiness	Righteousness
Dating	Jesus	Rock music
Death & Dying	Justice	Self-image
Discipleship	Judgment	Sex
Doubt	Legalism	Social concern
Drugs	Love	Scandal

Stealing	Trust	Wisdom
Suicide	Unity	Witnessing
Television	Values	Worldliness
Temptation	War	Worry
Touching	Will of God	Worship

RECORDING ILLUSTRATIONS FROM YOUR PERSONAL BIBLE STUDY

The impact of your personal Bible study and relationship with the Lord will give you many excellent illustrations. Although it is not always wise to use your own experience as a resource, there are times when your own struggles and growth bring life to the message or speech you are giving.

As you conduct your personal Bible study and prayer time, keep a journal of your discoveries and of God's faithfulness in your own life. Be sure to include dates, sources, and exact biblical references. Type each insight or illustration on standard paper. Make enough copies of each one to match the topics it could fit. Then file them under that topic. Some will fit only one topic. Others could fit several.

For example, an illustration about forgiveness might also fit under guilt and freedom. Although this requires some thought and time, it is well worth the effort. Perhaps long after you have forgotten the actual illustration, you may prepare a message on guilt. If you go to the file on guilt you will find the illustration you need. Even though forgiveness was the context in which you first discovered the illustration, because you took the time to classify it under guilt, it will be there when you need it. If you had filed it only under forgiveness you would never find it for other applications.

RECORDING ILLUSTRATIONS FROM MAGAZINES

When the illustration is from a magazine or other written source there is no need to retype it. Tear the article from the magazine, make enough copies to fit the number of topics that apply, and file appropriately. Remember to credit speakers you are quoting and include publication and article titles, authors of the magazine articles you file, dates, and publishing information. Your credibility is enhanced by giving references to sources of the material. It also gives the audience a change to research your topic in more detail.

Do not give in to the temptation to keep illustrations written on napkins, matchbook covers, and envelopes. I can speak from experience in saying you will never be able to find them when you need them. You will search endlessly for the napkin with barbecue sauce stain that contains the perfect illustration for Wednesday's presentation. Always transfer your observations from your notebook to typewritten form and file them as soon as possible.

RECORDING ILLUSTRATIONS FROM BOOKS

The process for recording illustrations found in books follows a slightly different progression that will allow you to keep the best of the book without destroying the enjoyment of your reading. I owe my thanks to Jim Green for this system.

1. Read with the eye of the hunter.

2. Put a *pencil* check in the margin beside passages that strike you as significant.

3. Record the page number on the inside of the back cover of the book and continue reading. You need to record the page number only once, even if there is more than one passage checked on that page (see Figure 1).

Figure 1

4. Review all checked passages after you have finished the book. Some of the passages will no longer seem relevant because they are not being read in the context of the book. They will not be relevant to the listener either. If the passage can stand alone as an illustration, leave the check; if not, erase it.

5. Type the name of the book, author, page number, date of publication, and city and name of the publisher at the top of a standard sheet of paper. Then type each of the passages. At the head of each significant passage,

type the page number followed by the number of topics to which the passage applies (see Figure 2).

LIFE AMONG THE LIVING
Jeff Wilson
Judas Publication House:

Page 3   TOPIC(S)   Curiosity / Sex
The small boy dissected a frog to find out what made it jump, but in learning something about the parts he destroyed its life.

Page 6   TOPIC(S)   Commitment / Sin / Loneliness When she looked back, he was gone! If only she had been move loving. Now she was alone....

Figure 2

6. Photocopy the entire document. Make enough photocopies of each illustration to fit the number of topics. Some will fit under one topic and others will require several. Keep the original and cut the photocopied document into strips each containing one illustration. Keep the original document folded in the back of the book. There will be times when you cannot find an illustration in your file but you will remember the book it came from. A quick review of the paper in the back will yield the illustration you are searching for.

It takes a lot of time to find and file illustrations correctly, but the effort will be rewarded many times over by the freshness and power evident in your speeches.

Chapter Six

PUTTING IT ALL TOGETHER

Once you understand how to plan and organize your speeches, the next step is to organize your life so that you can prepare consistently good speeches. This chapter deals with three skills that can enhance the power of your communication by helping you "put it all together." The skills covered in this chapter are the following: learning to manage your time, applying the principle of one ahead, and learning to think in outline form.

LEARN TO MANAGE YOUR TIME

One day a bright young pastor raised his hand at the conclusion of a four-day seminar. "The material that I have learned here is invaluable," he said. "My problem is that I can't afford the time to prepare each of my talks with such meticulous care."

Knowing that he had to prepare several talks each week I understood his frustration. However my response was not what he expected. I told him, "You can't afford not to take the time to prepare your talks with care."

I would extend the same challenge to you. Whether you are a Sunday school teacher, pastor, youth worker, or public speaker, if your message is important, you should give it your best effort in preparation and delivery. If your message is not worth that effort, it's probably not worth presenting. If you are speaking so often that you don't have time to prepare your talks, you are speaking too often.

That brings us around to the skill of managing time. The biggest reason why people don't think they have the time to prepare adequately is that they have never learned to manage their time. As a result they operate under an emergency system called crisis management. Crisis management is the approach you used back in high school when you waited until just before an assignment was due before beginning to work on it.

If you find yourself preparing for a Sunday school lesson on Friday, Saturday, or Sunday you are operating under crisis management. If you begin to prepare a sermon the same week it's to be delivered, you are operating under crisis management. This kind of management under-mines the potential of every talk you give. It robs it of beautiful illustrations and research that could bring power and credibility to what will otherwise be a mediocre talk.

Just two simple steps to time management can change that. First, you must understand that the cost of saving time is time. In the long run the SCORRE system will save you time in preparation. However you must be willing to invest the time up front to make it work. Here's what that investment will cost you. If you speak on a weekly basis and want to be as excellent as possible in your preparation, you should get away at least three days each quarter to plan ahead.

Are you willing to take the time away from your everyday responsibilities to plan for excellence in the messages and speeches you will be giving in the coming months? The common response is, "I would love to do that, but I'm just too busy." There is a hidden fear that everyday needs would go unmet and your ministry or business would fall apart.

I bet you can look back on a time in your life when sickness or emergency took you away from work for several days. When you returned, had your ministry crumbled or your business gone bankrupt? No! You probably picked up where you left off with hardly a blink. If sickness can take you from your work for two or three days without significant damage, imagine what three days of concentrated planning can do to enhance your speaking.

The wise money manager knows that if he wants to make money over a period of time he must be willing to invest some money up front. You will never get beyond crisis management until you are willing to invest some time up front regularly. If you are willing to commit to that investment, you can reap wonderful dividends in your communication.

APPLY THE PRINCIPLE OF ONE AHEAD

A speech is like a good wine. The best are those that have had a chance to ferment and age. A good host would never serve a wine that had been in the bottle for only a week. Likewise there is no excuse for serving up a message that has not had time to ferment.

There are four stages to any speech, sermon, or talk.

The first stage is the *idea* stage where the speech is just a gleam in your eye. A portion of Scripture has caught your attention. You have decided to address a need but have not yet determined a specific focus. Or you have chosen a subject but haven't yet focused on what aspect of that subject you are going to cover. In this stage of development your talk has not taken shape. At most you have a few ideas on paper at the end of it.

Next comes what I call the *skeleton* stage. During this stage you work your idea through the SCORRE process. You write an objective sentence and the points of your rationale. By the end of it you've articulated exactly what you want to communicate, and you know how you are going to go about it.

The third stage of a speech is the *outline* stage. During this stage you add an opening and a closing and arrange your illustrations in outline form along with the objective sentence and rationale. You may even write out the speech in manuscript form.

It would be acceptable to deliver the speech at the end of this stage, but the excellent communicator would want the speech to go through one more process, the *fermentation* stage, during which the speech is allowed to ferment in the quiet cellars of your consciousness. Ideally every prepared speech should be given at least an additional week to interact with the enzymes of life. During this time you will encounter events and observations that fit perfectly with your speech. You will not be making major changes, but the additions and changes you do make will give your speech its final razor edge.

If you don't give your speech time to ferment, those events and observations will pass into oblivion without your ever being aware of their presence. If you allow your speech to ferment, they will become the powerful anecdotes, illustrations, and clarifications that raise your speech to the level of excellence. At that point you are ready to serve a *vintage* message.

The principle of *one* ahead means that you will begin working on speeches long before they are to be delivered and you will have them completed and fermenting at least one week ahead of time. The only way this will ever happen is if you make a commitment to get away and get ahead.

During the three or four days each quarter that you get away you should work exclusively on preparing three speeches in each of the stages mentioned above. You should consider not going back to work until you have one to three speeches in the outline stage and ready to ferment, three others in the skeleton stage awaiting outline development, and another three in the idea stage.

Start with the speech or speeches that need to be delivered first, and get them to the outline stage (ready to deliver). Next, work on the speeches that will be delivered at a later date and get them at least to the skeleton stage (objective sentence and rationale). You will find that these will do some fermenting as you wait to develop them further. Finally, put together some of the ideas that you are going to be working on for later speeches. Include not only the subject and central theme but also notes on how you might develop the speech to meet the needs of your audience.

When you get home you won't be working on just one message during your preparation time. Instead you'll have speeches in each of the stages, and you can work on bringing at least one speech from each stage forward.

For example you might deliver the speech on why the Christian should love his neighbor while the message on the importance of Bible study continues to ferment. You could develop the outline for your talk on discipline and begin fleshing out the embryo ideas for your speech on witnessing (to be delivered in several weeks). Then you can write down your emerging thoughts about the Christian approach to the New Age movement (still in the idea stage). The following week you will be putting this very talk in skeleton form and adding to the idea column a new theme that needs to be developed.

This way of working keeps you from always preparing at the last minute for the talk you are suppose to give in a few days. Even if you can't allow the finished product to ferment for a week, it will be doing so during the entire process of development. In the long run this kind of graduated planning and development will not only result in better deliveries, it will save you time.

STAGES OF PREPARATION

	Idea EMBRYO IDEAS	Skeleton OBJECTIVE SENTENCE & RATIONALE	Outline FULL OUTLINE OPENING CLOSING ILLUSTRATIONS	Fermentation Fine Tune	Delivery
Week One	New Age	Witnessing	Discipline	Bible Study	Loving Your Neighbor (This message was in preparation the previous week.)
Week Two	Romans 12	New Age	Witnessing	Discipline	Bible Study
Week Three	New Idea	Romans 12	New Age	Witnessing	Discipline

Each week each speech is moved to the next stage of preparation

Figure 1

LEARN TO THINK IN OUTLINE FORM

When you SCORRE a speech by writing an objective sentence and rationale, you should think of that as the heart of your speech. See Figure 1. That sentence and the rationale that supports it contain the focal point for everything that will happen from the time you step to the platform until you sit down. But you will actually say more than just what is contained in that skeletal structure. You will still need some kind of opening to prepare the audience to hear what you are going to say, and a closing that will burn it into their minds and hearts for days, if not years, to come.

The actual outline of your entire talk has three major parts. The first part is the opening, the last part is the closing, and sandwiched between is the heart of your message: SCORRE. This outline in Figure 2 has two important functions.

First of all, *it keeps you organized*. Anything that does not lead to the objective of the speech will not fit well in the outline.

Second, *it keeps you on time*. If you use the blanks to the left of the outline to give each part of the speech a time value it will help you prepare and deliver a balanced speech.

I can't tell you how many times I have labored over an important message, afraid that I might not have enough material, and then ended up running out of time on my first point. The fear of not having enough to say causes many speakers to prepare too much material. Once they are behind the pulpit or podium the adrenaline takes over, they wax eloquent on the introduction or first couple of points, only to realize too late that there is no time left to give the rest of the speech.

As you outline your speech, estimate how much time you have to spend on each part, then prepare the most convincing material to fill that allotment and stick to the limits you set for yourself. The total time you are allotted is not going to grow just because you took most of it for your introduction.

Figure 2 shows a more detailed description of each part of the outline.

The Opening

Use the opening of your speech to get the audience to want to hear what you are going to say. At this crucial juncture, they will decide whether they will listen to you or not. If your opening fails to grab their interest, chances are slim that you will win them back later.

Before a farmer can plant a seed, he must prepare the soil to receive it. Before a speaker can communicate, he must break through the "what have you got to say that is of interest to me" attitude and take control. You must make the audience understand why you want to talk to them and make them believe that it is important to them. Each group will require a different approach, but in general your opener has two functions: to gain the attention of the audience and to stimulate their interest in the content of your talk.

Putting It All Together

---

30 Minutes
Four skills to better parenting

7:00PM ——————— 5 MIN —— [OPENING]

ATTENTION GETTER

1 MIN Story: Where did I come from?

INTRODUCTION

4 MIN The need for better parenting

1 MIN * Other parents' frustrations
1 MIN * Personal frustrations
1 MIN * National Survey: 81% need help
1 MIN * The shopping story

7:05PM ——————— 20 MIN —— [SCORRE]

1 MIN The solution: Transition into objective of talk

We all want to be better parents. Tonight I would like to identify 4 skills that will help us achieve that goal.

(Every parent can be more effective by developing 4 parenting skills.)

5 MIN 1.   Develop a sense of humor
    1 MIN A. Norman Cousins quote
    2 MIN B. Jesus' example. Mt. 19:24; 23:24
    2 MIN C. Definition: Parallel to gospel message.

5 MIN 2.   Develop a spirit of forgiveness
    2 MIN A. Survey: "I'm sorry. I was wrong."
    1 MIN B. Christ's attitude. Lk. 23:24; Col. 3:13
    2 MIN C. Story: Teenage prostitute

3 MIN 3.   Develop an attitude of encouragement
    2 MIN A. Story: The gold miner
    1 MIN B. Personal illustration: H. S. teacher

6 MIN 4.   Develop an atmosphere of trust
    3 MIN A. Trust your child. Expect the best.
    3 MIN B. Trust God. He cares more than you do.

7:25PM ——————— 5 MIN —— [CLOSING]

1 MIN REVIEW: Objective and rationale

3 MIN APPLICATION: What steps will you take to develop these skills? Introduce "Family Feud" parenting class starting January 7.

7:30pm _1 MIN_ Prayer: For strength to respond to God's leading

---

Although this outline means little to the casual reader, the phrases and words remind the well-prepared speaker of illustrations, quotes, and other points that flesh out the speech.

Figure 2

The Attention-Getter

The attention-getter is important because it is lets you establish contact and take control.

I recently asked our youth pastor how he got the attention of his junior high students so he could communicate truth. "When they come into the room," he said, "they are so full of energy that they can hardly sit still. I have forty-five minutes of class time. We play wild games and use a lot of group dynamics for forty minutes. At the end of that time they are worn out just enough so that they stop for a breath of air and look up. At that moment," he declared, "I have five minutes to drive home the *heart* of my message."

Our youth director, wisely, uses forty minutes of opening to get the attention of that energetic crowd and prepare them to hear a powerful, if short message. Now, I doubt that you would have to open with forty minutes of broom hockey to win the right to be heard by a group of senior citizens or a Sunday morning congregation, but it is an excellent strategy for capturing the attention of a junior high energy machine with a five-minute attention span.

The way you approach the front will have a major effect on gaining the attention of your audience. Whether you are walking to the pulpit, stepping to the lectern at a business function, or taking a stand in front of a group of teenagers, you should approach that position with the attitude of a quarterback coming onto the football field. There is a job to be done and you are the one in charge.

The sense of command and confidence in your voice as you say "Good evening" can be all that it takes to let the audience know that you want their attention, and an anecdote or humorous story delivered with enthusiasm may be just the thing to gain you a hearing. If your demeanor and first words get their attention, what follows must quickly convince them that you *deserve* their attention.

The Introduction

> The introduction is only the porch the listener must cross to get into the main house. The speaker should not keep his audience waiting on the porch. He should usher them into the house as soon as convenient (Lloyd Perry, *Manual for Biblical Preaching*, 77).

The introduction should make very clear what the focus of the message is going to be. No unrelated jokes or stories here. A good introduction should stir interest in the content of your talk. At this point in the talk, what each member of the audience wants to know more than anything else is "What is this talk going to be about and what does it have to do with me?" Too often the speaker doesn't give even a clue.

You should use the introduction to state your objective clearly and leave your audience eager for more.

If I stepped in front of a group of business people in a large office building and began to describe three routes that would enable them to leave the building in less than one minute, chances are I would lose their attention almost immediately.

If, however, I present my message in a way that conveys a sense of urgency that is compelling, you can get a captive audience. Consider this introduction.

> Ladies and gentlemen, there's a fire on the lower floors. *The only way you can survive is to leave the building within sixty seconds. I will give you three routes you can take that will save your life.*

Notice that I clearly stated the objective in conversational English:

> Every *person* can *survive this fire by taking one of three ROUTES.*

With an introduction like that, the audience wants to know "What routes?"

Often I give a message entitled "How to get the most out of life." I quote a familiar beer commercial as an attention-getter. (Believe me, it works.) The commercial begins with the words, "You only go around once, so you've got to reach for all the gusto you can get." The commercial suggests that you can get all of the gusto out of life by drinking beer.

In my introduction I draw attention to the fact that we really do go around only once (regardless of what Shirley MacLaine may say) and that most men and women want to live life to its fullest potential. We want to get all the gusto there is to get. Since we agree that drinking beer won't bring that quality of life, what will? As a transition to the content of my message I say, "Today I would like to reveal three principles you can live by that will allow you to live to the fullest potential for which you where created. Those principles are: live with nothing to prove, nothing to hide, and nothing to lose."

The identification with the beer ad grabs attention, and the promise of a formula for quality living creates the interest.

Sometimes the attention-getter and the introduction are contained in the same phrase. "You can learn to hate God, and tonight I'm going to show you how." This introduction will grab attention for a talk on those things that cause us to turn our back on God.

Here is an overview of information relevant to a good opener in outline form. (I am indebted to Lloyd Perry's *Manual* for much of the outline below.)

A. Ingredients of a Good Opener
  1. An attention-getter
  2. An introduction
  3. A smooth transition to the SCORRE'd message

B. Purpose of the Opener
  1. Establish contact with the listener (attention-getter)
  2. Develop positive rapport
  3. Stir interest in the text or topic
  4. Give a basis for giving the talk
  5. Make the audience want to listen
  Purposes 1, 3, and 5 are essential in every opener.

C. Qualities of a Good Opener
  1. Brief
  2. Clear
  3. Appropriate
  4. Purposeful

   5. Audience-centered

D. Characteristics of a Poor Opener
1. Full of flattery
2. Apology-ridden
3. Predictable
4. Complex
5. Without purpose

E. Optional Ingredients of a Good Opener
1. Startling statement
2. Question
3. Quotation
4. Humorous story
5. Word picture
6. Comparison
7. Discovery
8. Statement of problem
9. Visual aid
10. Proposition*
11. Prediction
12. Current event
13. Observation
14. Dramatic description
15. A conundrum

---

* Your objective sentence should be a part of every introduction. As a proposition it serves very well as the transition to the heart of the message.

16. A paradox
17. A Scripture reading
18. A definition

THE HEART OF THE SPEECH

This is the focused presentation you planned, using the SCORRE process. In its full outline form it will now include illustrations and data not included when you simply had an objective statement and rationale.

In the opening you catch the attention and interest of the audience. In the heart of the message you must deliver. Everything you do and say before you get to the heart should prepare the way for this message. Everything you will say in your conclusion will relate to the heart. The minute you lose sight of the singular focus and central importance of this part of your talk, you will defuse its potential power.

THE CONCLUSION

There is a saying in show business that goes, "You're only as good as your last performance." The same can be said for a speech. "You're only as good as the last words you say!" Millions of good speeches have been ruined by long, drawn out, inconclusive endings. Whenever I hear the words "and in conclusion," I cringe because many times it signals the beginning of another speech.

The basic purposes of a conclusion are to summarize the rationale and objective of your talk, give opportunity for

application or response, and burn the focus into the hearts and minds of the listeners. The old saw that goes "Tell 'em what you're going to say, say it, and then tell 'em what you've said" really is valid. The opening is where you tell them what you are going to say, the heart is where you say it, and the conclusion provides the opportunity to review what you have said. On the surface it may seem simplistic, but in practice it works. A brief summary of your logic should be a part of every conclusion.

Using the conclusion to allow the audience to respond to a message solves a common frustration.

Consider a message with this objective:

> True evangelism is obligatory in nature.

Based on this objective, we could prepare a message that persuades the audience of their need for Christ. But shouldn't we also include in our SCORRE'd message, rationale that show the audience how to receive Christ? The answer is a resounding *no!* Efforts to do so will serve only to dilute the power of persuasion. Yes, you should give them opportunity to respond and instructions on how to do so, but that should be done in the conclusion. The heart of the message is singularly obligatory in nature. How to receive Christ is not a complicated message, and it is the natural application for a person who has been convicted of his or her need to receive him.

Much confusion results when students try to work into their SCORRE'd objective and rationale what should be a part of the conclusion. Your conclusion should give opportunity for application. Those who have listened to a theological message can be challenged to further study. Other messages offer opportunity to respond with specific action. Altar calls and public response are most appropriate in the conclusion, but unless you have convinced your audience of the need for action, it is pointless at this juncture suddenly to preach another sermon or give another talk.

The following information will help you summarize the elements of a good conclusion:

A. Purpose of the Conclusion
   1. To restate the objective and remind the listener of the logic that led to that objective (should be part of every conclusion)
   2. To give opportunity for practical application
   3. To summarize the talk

B. Qualities of a Good Conclusion
   1. Brief
   2. Clear
   3. Unifying
   4. Well-prepared
   5. Appropriate
   6. Practical
   7. Memorable

C. Characteristics of a Poor Conclusion
   1. Long and drawn out
   2. Unrelated to the message

3. Weak and unmemorable
4. Without summary of rationale and proposition
5. Another message

D. Optional Components of a Conclusion

1. Summary
2. Quotation
3. Exhortation
4. Brief story or illustration
5. Prayer
6. Public response
7. Suggested course of action
8. Striking statement
9. Appeal for consideration
10. Challenge to application

Chapter Seven

INVOLVING THE AUDIENCE

The last chapter dealt with three skills that can help you put it all together. In this chapter we will deal with another important skill, one that will help you establish a link with your audience as you speak.

I used to be enthralled with the old philosophical riddle that asked, "If a tree falls in the forest and no one hears it, does it make a sound?" Some would argue that sound becomes sound only when the atmospheric disturbance we know as sound waves actually hits the ear and is perceived as sound. Before that time it is only potential sound.

The same argument can be applied to communication. If a speaker speaks and there is no one there to hear (or if no one chooses to listen), communication does not take place. Some have gone so far as to say that communication does not take place until the listener is moved to action. The point is that the audience is an essential part of the communication equation.

Often as we prepare we are so concerned about doing well that we forget the other half of the communication team, the audience. Without them there can be no communication. To be successful, the speaker must touch his audience. The more they are involved in the communication process, the more attentive they will be and the longer they will retain what they hear.

According to an article in *Bottom Line* magazine, "The human brain gets 87 percent of its information from the eyes and only 9 percent from the ears" (March 30, 1985, p. 6).

Pedagogues in England suggest that we remember 10 percent of what we hear, 30 percent of what we see, 60 percent of what we see and hear, and 80 percent of what we see, hear, and do.

Although the least effective method of communication is straight lecture, this is the method we have chosen to communicate the most important message on the face of the earth. Jesus often used object lessons, visual aids, and physical demonstrations as he taught. His miracles were not parlor tricks to entertain the crowds; they were demonstrations of the truths he was teaching and ulti-mately a demonstration of his deity.

In this chapter I will give you ideas on how you can bring your talk from the level of a lone tree falling in the woods to its fullest potential as a crashing roar of truth in the ears of your listeners.

Unfortunately, you might not be able to put all these actions to use. You may be limited by the traditions of your church. Your audience might be shocked to see any-thing changed from the comfortable norm.

In my workshops, I often make the point that you can be more effective as a speaker if you are willing to step out from behind the pulpit. One time a pastor from a very formal church approached me afterward. "I would love to use many of your suggestions in our worship," he said. "But if I so much as change the order in our bulletin I am brought before the board to explain my actions."

I am not suggesting that you shock your church into relieving you of your duties. You may not have the freedom to implement all of the actions suggested below, but that doesn't change the fact that they can dramatically change the quality of your communication. Use what you can and move slowly to gain acceptance. Remember, no matter how effective the method, if it offends your audience its effectiveness is nullified.

INVOLVE YOUR AUDIENCE IN PLANNING YOUR SPEECH

As you prepare your speech, the audience should never be far from your mind. After all, the objective you have worked so hard to develop has meaning only as it relates to this group of people. Pastors, teachers, and youth workers will find that each week virtually the same people hear their message. Yet each week that same group of people make up a different audience. One week they'll be festive and jubilant, and the next they'll be introspective and quiet. Those changes can happen even between morning and evening of the same day. In fact, if you deliver a boring talk, their mood may change even while you speak.

If you speak to the same people week after week, try, as you prepare, to anticipate what they will be like this week. What current events or community affairs are affecting their thinking? What is happening within your church or organization that is affecting attitudes? The object is not to guess the exact mood of your audience or to determine the specific needs of every person in the audience, but to keep them in mind throughout the entire preparation process.

When you are invited to speak, find out what age the audience will be, and what kind of programming will precede your presentation. Ask your host to give you some insight into the personality of the people you will be addressing. Are they reserved, intellectual, fun-loving?

Occasionally an audience's attitude will change during a meeting. If that happens you may not necessarily want to change your speech, but you had better be prepared to adjust the mood of your presentation. You will always want to start where they are.

Just before I got up to speak at a Sunday evening youth service, my audience watched a beautiful multimedia presentation set to the music of "How Great Thou Art." When the lights came back on, there was not a dry eye in the place. Up to that time the mood had been one of celebration and praise, but the media presentation had quickly and effectively changed the mood to quiet worship. I had planned to begin my talk with several funny stories to win them over, but now that no longer seemed right for the spirit of the audience. The Spirit of God had already used another medium to win them over, so I opened with a few moments of silent prayer and moved directly into the message I had prepared.

Involve your audience from the beginning of your preparation all the way through the delivery of your talk. They are the focus of your communication.

INVOLVE YOUR AUDIENCE IN THINKING

Involving your audience in thinking is not the same thing as making them guess what in the world you are trying to say. An unfocused presentation will make them think all right. But not about your talk. Minds will soon begin to wander and think about the tasks that need to be done at home or the business deal that needs to be closed.

One of the greatest actions you can take to involve your audience in thinking is to provide them with the skeleton outline of your talk or sermon. Unfortunately bulletins usually highlight the order of worship and neglect to help the congregation worship by showing them the order of the message. The same kind of outline is helpful for Sunday school classes and youth meetings.

I have had several students ask me if providing the outline for a sermon wouldn't oversimplify the presentation. One young man even suggested that his intellectual congregation would be offended by such simplicity. Months later I got a letter from him saying that the reaction of his people had been far from critical. His focused speaking as the result of SCORRE and his willingness to allow the audience to follow his thinking inspired one of the research scientists in his congregation to write a note that said, "Finally, you are making sense."

Fancy titles for a talk have never kept the attention of any person in the audience. Simple outlines of the heart of your talk help hold interest because they tend to make your audience anticipate the development of that outline.

You can make the outline from a presentable form of your objective sentence and the rationale to support it. Leave room between elements of your rationale for the audience to take notes on the details of your delivery.

Here's how that could work. Let's suppose your objective sentence reads:

> Every person can test the will of God by following three steps given by Paul in Romans 12:1-2.

The corresponding outline might look like the one below. Remember to keep it simple. You don't need to preach the entire sermon in the outline.

> Three steps to knowing the will of God
> Romans 12:1-2
>
> 1. Give God your body: Romans 12:1
> 2. Give God your will: Romans 12:2a
> 3. Give God your mind: Romans 12:2b
>
> Food for Thought
>
> How much are you willing to give God?
> What is it that you are holding back?
> What can you give him today?
> Are you willing to take the three steps suggested by Paul?

Don't be afraid to let your audience know what to look for. Near the beginning of almost all my presentations I will make a statement like this: "Today I have one purpose in stepping before you, to give you three reasons why you should commit your life totally to a loving Christ."

Now they know the purpose of my talk and the method I am going to use to persuade them: I am trying to convince them to commit their lives to Christ, and I am going to give them three reasons why they should do so. This kind of message makes the listener look forward with anticipation to hear what the reasons might be. Even a hostile person will listen so that he might refute those reasons.

If possible, offer one or two classes in which you teach your audience what to look for in your presentations. Teach them to look for a clear and pinpointed objective and organized, convincing rationale to support it.

A good way to tell how well you are doing at communicating is to ask a friend or two after a talk to repeat back to you what you tried to communicate. Assure them that you are not testing to see whether they were listening, that you want to know how successful you were at communicating. You will find it an enlightening exercise, and it will make you want to work harder at involving your audience.

LET YOUR AUDIENCE SEE WHAT YOU ARE SAYING

When properly used, visual aids make a lasting and powerful impact on the audience.

In a formal church, I heard a message I will never forget. The speaker was talking about the diseases that destroy a church. He had printed the name of each of the diseases neatly on a white card just large enough so the entire congregation could read it. He had then placed the cards to the left of the pulpit on a small easel. To the right of the pulpit, he placed a small stand holding a beautiful porcelain model of a church. As he finished talking about each of the diseases he would move that card to the back of the stack revealing the next disease. At the conclusion of his message the pastor took all the cards from the easel and swept the delicate little church from the table.

The sight and sound as it shattered on the floor remains in my memory. More important, so are the names of the diseases that destroyed it. They were lack of worship, lack of fellowship, lack of stewardship, lack of commitment, and lack of forgiveness.

But the preacher was not finished. As quickly as the pieces of that church came to rest, he reached into the pulpit, pulled out another card, and set it on the stand. "Which," he asked, "do you want our church to be? Like all churches we have some of the diseases that can destroy us. Next week I will preach on biblical steps we can take to keep that from happening."

"Oh no!" I thought, "a 'to-be-continued' sermon." I could not attend that service since I was to be hundreds of miles away the next Sunday, but he had piqued my interest and I requested a tape. The next Sunday, he put an odd-shaped piece of material on the pedestal with each card. At the end of the sermon he had built a sturdy little church from these pieces of material. I wish I could have been there.

The tasteful use of visual aids within the boundaries of what your situation will allow can bring staying power to the focus of your message and make your audience want to be there.

INVOLVE YOUR AUDIENCE IN WRITING

I think one of the greatest compliments a speaker can receive is to see the audience writing. I often encourage my audience to write down the rationale to the message as I give it. This keeps them on track with the logic of your message and encourages you to make sure they understand as you move from rationale to rationale. Provide space and pencils so that your audience can keep a record of your presentation. From time to time, your talk may trigger tangential ideas in the minds of your listeners. If they can write these thoughts down it will serve two objectives. First, it allows them to record the thought so they can pursue it at a later time. Second, because they are confident they will not forget that thought, they can give full attention to the rest of your message.

INVOLVE YOUR AUDIENCE IN HEARING

I highly recommend that people who make their living by speaking record every message that they give. By replaying your talk, you'll be able to see where you need to sharpen your skills. Videotaping is even better.

Another reason for recording your messages is to make them available to your listeners for further listening. If I hear a message that is particularly challenging or one that I want to consider more carefully, I will always get a tape if it is available. If you simply make it known that you have such tapes, people will ask for them.

INVOLVE YOUR AUDIENCE VOCALLY

One of the most powerful tools in teaching and speaking is to allow the audience to respond verbally. Even the old and familiar *Amen* is an action that affirms to the preacher that the audience has heard and agrees.

Why not have the audience repeat the rationale of the message? Why not have the audience be free to ask questions? Remember, if you are leaving some big question unanswered in the minds of your audience, they will not get any further in your message than where they first became aware of the unresolved question.

I have been in church services, youth meetings, and Sunday school classes where questioning is allowed without destroying the flow or purpose of the talk, and I can testify that the attention level of the audience is remarkable in these situations. Even the simple act of asking the audience to repeat the rationale as you finish can make a big difference.

After speaking to a large group using the crystal clear focusing techniques of SCORRE as presented in this book, I was still disappointed to find that many could not remember the purpose or rationale of my talk. I resolved that I would find a way to burn the essence of that talk into the minds of my listeners. The next time I had the opportunity to give this talk I began with an objective statement just as I had before.

"You can believe that you are a valuable individual in the eyes of God," I said. I reminded the audience of the thousands of inner city kids who had responded to the message of Jessie Jackson as he traveled to high schools and had them repeat the phrase: "I am somebody."

I asked my audience to repeat that phrase: "If you really believe that you are valuable in the eyes of God you can say with confidence 'I am somebody.'" The audience was reluctant at first, but soon they were shouting "I am somebody."

I then gave them three reasons that they could confidently make that claim. Each time I finished giving one of the reasons I had the audience repeat it and tie it to the objective. I am somebody because God created me unique. I am somebody because God loves me. And so on.

I was not totally comfortable with this style and it was obvious that the audience was not used to responding. But their quick enthusiasm convinced me to continue. The survey that followed that message revealed that 80 percent of the audience knew that they were valuable individuals in the eyes of God and could remember all of the reasons why. You may not be able to have your group shouting enthusiastic answers as this group did, but if you can understand that your audience will retain the important aspects of your talk much longer if they voice them, then whenever possible you can give them the opportunity to do so.

INVOLVE YOUR AUDIENCE IN ACTION

Nothing will imprint the truth of your message more firmly in the hearts of your audience than if you give them the opportunity to act on what they have heard. In

Charles M. Sheldon's book, *In His Steps*, it was the people who acted on Pastor Henry Maxwell's sermon whose lives were changed.

Whenever possible you ought to provide opportunity for your audience to apply what you have been teaching. If you challenge your audience to demonstrate the love of Christ in their homes, suggest possible actions that will give them the chance to see how such love will affect their family. A youth group that is challenged to show concern for the less fortunate should be given the opportunity to paint a house, clean a yard, or visit children in the hospital.

I remember how frustrated I would get when I was told of the needy people in the world but was never given any practical suggestions as to how I could make a difference. I knew in my heart that going without hamburger on Thursday really wasn't going to feed anyone. Then one day Ron Sider, author of *Rich Christians in an Age of Hunger*, suggested several actions I could take that would make a difference.

It is important to note that he did not preach another sermon. His comments were part of a brief but powerful conclusion. He didn't stop there. For those of us who wanted further information he scheduled another session that would give specific details on the actions we could take. At that session he gave an enabling message. I filled a notebook with material that I still use as a reference today. Because I am living the principles that he taught, I could not forget them if I tried.

Some messages lend themselves to application and action better than others. If you are teaching on the persons of the Trinity, you can't very well ask folks to go home and do the Holy Spirit. But you can encourage your audience to do further reading and provide a bibliography or make the books available. There is always room for application.

If you involve your audience, it will move you into a new realm of communication. Instead of treating your talks like performances, the audience will become a part of your messages. It is almost as if they take part in the presenting of the message.

This is the kind of communication that Jesus used constantly in his ministry. He withered fig trees, changed water into wine, and raised the dead to demonstrate that he was truly the Son of God. He continually asked his disciples and converts to take action so that they might see the power of God demonstrated in their lives.

To the adulterous women he said, "Go and sin no more." He asked the blind man to go wash the mud from his eyes, and he asked the fishermen to cast their nets on the other side of the boat. He told his disciples to love each other with the same unconditional love that he had demonstrated toward them, and he asked his disciples difficult questions that caused them to ponder the focus of his message.

It is not easy to involve your audience. It requires careful, creative preparation, absolute commitment to preach truth rather than opinion, and constant caution not to let the technique diffuse the focus of the message. In the long run, though, increased interest, retention, and under-standing makes it worth the effort.

Chapter Eight

USING SCORRE TO TEACH
AND PREACH SCRIPTURE

This chapter deals specifically with the SCORRE process as it relates to preaching and teaching directly from Scripture texts. It is for the benefit of all who present scriptural truth.

There is no need to twist Scripture to get it to fit the SCORRE principles taught in this book. Remember that the two primary functions of the SCORRE process are to keep the speaker focused and to help the speaker make a logical and organized presentation. The authors of Scripture wrote with an objective in mind and most presented their thoughts in an organized and logical fashion. In fact, the SCORRE process is helpful in uncovering the author's objectives.

Webster defines homiletics as "the science that teaches the principles of adapting the discourses of the pulpit to the spiritual benefit of the hearers." Without good homiletics it is possible to present a discourse from the pulpit that is not spiritually beneficial to the hearer. The most common error is to rumble through a portion of Scripture saying something about each of the subjects it touches upon. The temptation to include too much is especially strong when presenting expository messages.

I heard a congressman submit his audience to this torture in a recent speech. "There are so many good things that I want to talk about tonight," he droned, "that I have decided to ramble a bit and talk about all of them." Unlike many politicians, this one kept his word. The next hour was a boring and ineffectual rambling that went nowhere.

Out of a genuine motivation to give people the best, many pastors and teachers take a portion of the Word of God and try to bring to the audience all of the good things presented in that text. SCORRE helps the speaker choose a single objective and present it with power.

Before beginning this chapter it is important to identify briefly what I perceive to be the difference between textual and topical preaching. Textual preaching is the interpretation of the meaning, intent, and possible application of a particular portion of Scripture. The limitations and boundaries of such a message are defined by the passage itself. Topical preaching, on the other hand, is the interpretation and expansion of a biblical topic or truth, and is not necessarily confined to one specific passage. The topical message is limited only by the scope of the chosen subject and the confines of the biblical truth.

Some would suggest that textual preaching is more spiritual and intellectually acceptable than topical preaching. I suggest that neither is more acceptable than the other and that both can be used to proclaim the message of Christ.

It is perhaps easier to abuse topical preaching. Too many topical messages have been prepared by developing the entire message based on the opinion of the speaker who then goes to Scripture to find a proof text. But this is a travesty. The best topical sermons are those that come as the result of the same good study principles that would be used to preach from a single text.

I have also seen many sermons labeled "textual" or "exegetical," which in truth are not. As Haddon Robinson aptly put it, "In many sermons the biblical passage read to the congregation resembles the national anthem played at a football game. It gets things started but is not heard again during the afternoon" (*Biblical Preaching*, [Baker, 1980], 20).

Here are seven basic steps that will enable you to use SCORRE to bring power to your preaching and teaching of Scripture.

STUDY

Study the Scriptures using the principles of good hermeneutics. Webster defines hermeneutics as "the science of interpretation, or of finding the meaning of an author's words and phrases and explaining it to others: particularly applied to the interpretation of the Scriptures." Although a passage of Scripture may have many applications, it has only one meaning. It is the responsibility of the speaker to use the principles of good hermeneutics to discover that meaning.

What does the passage say? This may be a foregone conclusion for those who have attended seminary and studied hermeneutics. However, it would be erroneous to conclude that only those who have attended seminary can understand and teach the Bible.

R. C. Sproul (*Knowing Scripture*, [InterVarsity, 1977], 13) addresses this as one of the myths that keep people from studying the Bible.

> Myth 1: The Bible is so difficult to understand that only highly skilled theologians with technical training can deal with the Scriptures.
>
> This myth has been repeated many times by sincere people. People say, "I know I can't study the Bible, because every time I try to read it, I can't understand it." When some people say that, they may want to hear, "That's all right. I understand. It's really a difficult book, and unless you've had seminary training, maybe you ought not to tackle it." Or perhaps they want to hear, "I know, it's too heavy, too deep, too profound. I commend you for your tireless efforts, your strenuous labors in trying to solve the mystifying riddle of God's Word. It is sad that God has chosen to speak to us in such obscure and esoteric language that only scholars can grasp it." This, I am afraid, is what many of us want to hear. We feel guilty and want to quiet our consciences for neglecting our duty as Christians [and teachers of the Word].

He goes on to say (p. 16),

> If you have been one of those who have clung to the myths of dullness or difficulty, perhaps it is because you have attributed to the whole of Scripture what you have found in some of its parts. Maybe some

passages have been peculiarly difficult and obscure. Other passages may have left you bewildered and baffled. Perhaps those should be left for the scholars to unravel.

I agree! But what are some of the basic study principles that you can follow? This is not meant to be a book on hermeneutics so I will not go into great detail on this subject. However, I would like to suggest the following principles as guidelines for those who are not familiar with Bible study techniques.

First, you should interpret the passage within the context of the book in which it appears. To whom was it written? For what purpose? Second, you should interpret the passage in question within the context of the whole message of the Bible. Third, you should consider the historical and cultural contexts, which can often shed light on the meaning of a passage. These principles help us understand what the Scripture is saying. Taken out of context the Scripture can be used to prove almost anything. Many of the cults use this technique to legitimize some very unscriptural concepts.

Unfortunately many well-meaning Christians do the same thing. For instance, it is a common error to apply some of the Old Testament promises made specifically to the nation of Israel to modern Christians. Although in principle God still cares for his people, it is not possible automatically to assume that all the promises God made to Israel are promises he made to us.

If you are not careful to keep the context of a passage foremost in your interpretation, you become vulnerable to errors that are far too common among those who teach and preach Scripture. For instance, many will go to great lengths to drag deep meaning out of every passage. They take a stab at the possible meaning of a difficult passage, take a passage out of context, or assign it a meaning that was never intended. These attempts to spiritualize a passage can distort it beyond recognition.

In my book, *How to Speak to Youth ... & Keep Them Awake at the Same Time*, I recounted a story from my youth that illustrates this practice.

> I remember once as a kid sitting in my Sunday school class with my cousin Jim. The teacher was discussing a Bible passage one phrase at a time and then asking members of the class to tell what they thought the phrase meant. The members of the class were parroting back to the teacher the kinds of answers she wanted to hear. Even at that young age, I couldn't believe what I was hearing.
>
> One boy was asked to explain the phrase "and the disciples left the house." Dutifully the boy thought for a moment and then in a quavering, religious voice, immortalized this bit of wisdom: "The four walls to the house represents four kinds of sin—the lust of the eyes, the lust of the flesh, the lust of money...." Here he paused. I could see he was running out of lusts. There were four walls; if this interpretation were to be good, he had to come up with one more lust, "...and the lust of lying," he continued. "When they walked out of the house, they escaped from the clutches of those lusts and from the evil of Satan, represented by the roof."

His face showed his obvious delight with that last bit of divine improvisation. He was richly praised for his interpretation of this portion of Scripture. My cousin was bent almost double trying to keep from bursting out in laughter. Seeing him about ready to explode, the teacher scowled, "Perhaps you have a better interpretation, Jim."

His face became sober, but I could still see a smile tugging at the corners of his mouth. Adopting the proper quavering voice, he said, "This is a verse that has touched my soul. When the Scripture (he even rolled the first r in Scripture the way some preachers do) says the disciples left the house, I believe that God is trying to tell us ..." (here he paused, looking heavenward) "... he's trying to tell us that the disciples left the house."

When the laughter died down and Jim had been properly dealt with for his smart-aleck answer, the class continued. But Jim was right. It didn't take a degree in Greek to know that the words were simply communicating that the disciples left the house. The kids in my Sunday school class were learning that the Bible was to be manipulated to say what we want it to say. Even at that age, many resented that approach and were growing to resent and mock the Scripture as well.

Another danger when you stray from the text is the temptation to propose something that is your opinion and pass it off as scriptural truth. Good hermeneutics will help you avoid these errors. For a more exhaustive look at hermeneutical principles, I recommend the following books as minimum requirement for those who teach and preach Scripture truth.

Knowing Scripture by R. C. Sproul, *Understanding Scripture* by A. Berkeley Mickelsen and Alvira M. Mickelsen, *New Testament Exegesis—A Handbook for Students and Pastors* by Gordon Fee, *How to Read the Bible for All It's Worth* by Gordon Fee and Douglas Stuart

LIST POSSIBLE SUBJECTS AND CENTRAL THEMES AND CHOOSE ONE

After you have unlocked the author's original meaning, you are ready to prepare your own sermon. Remember that although a passage has only one meaning, it may deal with several subjects and central themes. List the possible subjects and central themes as you study the passage and choose *just one!* Many textual sermons are dry and dusty because they present a continuous recitation of the Scripture without the opportunity to explore any one concept in depth. It's like rushing through a beautiful meadow without stopping to smell the flowers. You will not do a passage disservice by pausing to cover in detail one of the concepts taught there. Nor do you denigrate Scripture if you choose not to cover in one sitting every single concept that is taught. From your passage, pick a single subject and accompanying central theme using the methods we have taught in this book.

RECORD IDEAS THAT COME TO YOUR MIND THAT CAN BE USED FOR OTHER TALKS

The study of Scripture is so rich that it is difficult to avoid the temptation to include in your message everything that comes to your mind as you study. Gordon Fee explains the important difference between study methods and presentation methods.

> The immediate aim of the biblical student is to understand the biblical text. However, exegesis (it's a word used to describe investigation into the meaning of a biblical text) should not be an end in itself. Exegetical sermons are usually as dry as dust, informative perhaps, but seldom prophetic or inspirational. Therefore the ultimate aim of the biblical student is to apply one's exegetical understanding of the text to the contemporary church and the world. Thus this guide also includes some suggestions for moving from text to sermon, (*New Testament Exegesis: A Handbook for Students and Pastors* [Westminster, 1983], p. 21).

True exegesis is a method of study and not a method of presentation. It is a mistaken idea that you must bring the audience through the entire process of your study. If I don't understand Greek there is no need for me to go through every nuance of a word study to understand the meaning of a passage of Scripture. If it is a difficult or controversial passage that can be understood only by such examination, then fine, but there is no need to re-prepare the sermon with the audience. Just as a scientist brings to the public the results of his study in terms they can understand, so the proclaimer of the Word must present the results of study in the interesting and applicable format of a sermon.

You will find the SCORRE process of preparation particularly helpful in resisting the temptation to rehash every aspect of your study. Present the material that contributes to the focus of your message. So, what do you do with those fabulous gems that are uncovered as a result of your study but don't necessarily apply to the focus you have chosen? Save them for another message.

As you study and prepare never be without a notebook entitled "Ideas for Future Messages." Don't do a disservice to these gems by glossing over them quickly in a message where another focus commands attention. Record them in your notebook instead. On occasion you will even find the rough outline for another entire sermon.

DEVELOP THE OBJECTIVE

The next step is to use the SCORRE process to determine an objective for your talk. Be careful here. During this phase of the preparation it is possible to confuse the objective of the author with the objective of the speaker. Sometimes the objective revealed by Scripture will be clear and compelling, and when it is, you are obliged to prepare a message with that objective in mind. At other times, the author has written primarily to convey truth. Then it is acceptable for the speaker to develop an objective for the sermon that proclaims the truth offered in the passage and shows the audience the benefits that come to the believer from trusting in that truth. There are other times when subject, central theme, objective, and rational are provided right within the text.

Hebrews 4:14–16 is a good example of this. It reads:

> *Since we have a great high priest who has gone through the heavens, Jesus the Son of God, let us hold firmly to the faith we profess. For we do not have a high priest who is unable to sympathize with our weaknesses, but we have one who has been tempted in every way, just as we are—yet was without sin. Let us then approach the throne of grace with confidence, so that we may receive mercy and find grace to help us in our time of need.*

Subject: *The Priesthood of Christ*

Central theme: *The benefits of Christ's priesthood to the believer*

Objective: *Every Christian can receive mercy and find grace in time of need by taking advantage of the privileges made possible by Christ's priesthood.*

1. We can hold firmly to our faith (v. 14)

2. We can approach the throne with confidence (v. 16a)

Two questions will help you determine the objective for your message.

1. What aspect or application of this passage do I want to talk about?

2. Why do I want to talk about it?

Following are some examples drawn from John 13:

Example 1

Opening lines: "The subject of servanthood is obvious in John 13 so I want to talk about servanthood. Why? So people will be motivated to serve others."

The resulting objective would be obligatory:

Every person should be motivated to serve others because of two teachings found in John 13.

Example 2

Opening lines: "I want to talk about servanthood. Why? So people will know how much Christ loved them."

In this case the resulting objective would be enabling:

Every person can know the depths of Christ's love by understanding the three elements of servanthood demonstrated in John 13.

Example 3

Opening lines: "I want to talk about Christ's example of service found in John 13. Why? So that others will know the real meaning of service."

The resulting objective would be enabling but would have a different emphasis than the other two:

Every person can better know how to love others by following the examples set by Christ.

A. He loved in spite of circumstances.

B. He loved both friend and enemy.

C. His love was without limitation.

D. His love was a sign.

Example 4

Opening lines: "Since love is one of the themes of John 13, I want to talk about love. Why? So people will see its importance as a sign of Christianity."

The resulting objective represents a broader message of the passage:

Every person can understand the importance of love as the sign of a Christian by examining the actions of Christ in John 13.*

A. He said that it was a sign.

B. He demonstrated that it was a sign.

C. He commanded that we live it as a sign.

DETERMINE CONVINCING RATIONALE TO SUPPORT THE OBJECTIVE

From the Immediate Text

As we indicated previously, some Scripture contains the rationale in implied or written form right within the text. Romans 12:1–2 gives three steps the Christian can take to test and approve God's will.

---

* Note that what was once a supporting rationale for another objective (see D in Example 3) has become the proposition in this example. Scripture such as this is so rich with truth and its possible applications that you could preach for a month of Sundays and never leave the passage. As you study John 13 you will see that none of the above messages violates the intent or content of the text. Yet the speaker has the option of focusing the spotlight on one aspect of Jesus' proclamation and bringing it home to practical application for the believer.

I urge you, brothers, in view of God's mercy, to offer your bodies as living sacrifices, holy and pleasing to God—this is your spiritual act of worship. Do not conform any longer to the pattern of this world, but be transformed by the renewing of your mind. Then you will be able to test and approve what God's will is— his good, pleasing and perfect will (Romans 12:1–2, emphasis mine).

In verse 1 Paul implores the Christian to give his body to God. In verse 2 he says, "Do not conform any longer to the pattern of this world." And in the same verse he continues, "But be transformed by the renewing of your mind." And what is the result if the Christian decides to take Paul's advice? Paul finishes the passage by saying, "Then [if you do the above] you will be able to test and approve what God's will is—his good, pleasing, and perfect will."

These two verses of Scripture hold the outline for a fine sermon.

> Every Christian can test what God's will is by taking three steps of commitment.

1. Give your body to God.

2. Don't conform to this world.

3. Be transformed by the renewing of your mind.

The sermon might contain practical suggestions to show how Christians could take those steps in their daily lives. Should you choose to go into more detail, you could develop a separate outline on each rationale in preparation for a series of sermons.

Of course, not all passages of Scripture lend themselves so easily to the development of rationale. This is particularly true of narrative passages.

From Supportive Passages of Scripture

Let's continue with our example from Romans. Suppose you wanted to preach a message detailing the mercies of Christ to motivate the Christian to make his or her body a living sacrifice. You could draw the rationale from other passages in the book of Romans and the resulting objective might read like this:

> Every Christian should present his or her body as a living sacrifice because of the mercies of God.

The question that this objective brings to listeners' minds is: What mercies? To answer that question, you need to look at previous passages in Romans.

> Mercy #1: He has revealed his righteousness (chapter 1).
>
> Mercy #2: He has demonstrated his impartiality (chapters 1–3).
>
> Mercy #3: He has granted justification (chapters 3–5).
>
> Mercy #4: He has provided for our sanctification (chapters 6–8).
>
> Mercy #5: He has proved himself faithful (chapters 9–11).

FROM TRUTH THAT IS TAUGHT BY SCRIPTURE AS A WHOLE

Using the same passage, assume that your objective reads:

> Every person should offer his or her body to God as a living sacrifice for three reasons.

1. It is our spiritual act of worship.

2. It is the way we determine his perfect will.

3. It is what gives life meaning.

The third rationale is not found in the immediate text and may not be found in exactly those words anywhere in Scripture. But even an overview of Bible characters from Abraham to David to Paul will show that life took on meaning for many of these saints in direct relation to their commitment to a living God. Paul summarized this truth in his letter to the Philippians when he wrote, "For to me, to live is Christ and to die is gain" (1:21).

ADD ILLUSTRATIONS AND OTHER RESOURCES

Draw illustrations from personal experience and from biblical and extra-biblical sources to bring light and color to the truth taught by Scripture.

EVALUATE

It is important to evaluate and to be willing to make any necessary changes throughout the entire process. It is much easier to continue the preparation of a message simply because it must be finished than it is to insist on the academic and intellectual integrity that should be a part of every preparation evaluation.

Throughout your sermon preparation, you should constantly ask yourself the following questions:

Is my sermon true to scriptural truth?

Do I know what I am talking about?

Are my objective and the resulting outline crystal clear?

Am I living what I am preaching?

Will this message touch the needs of my audience?

How can I give them a way to respond?

IN CONCLUSION

The very nature of the SCORRE process makes it an excellent tool for Bible study and the preparation of expositional messages. Follow the seven steps as you prepare your next textual message and discover how it helps you identify the objectives of the author and keeps you focused in your presentation.

Chapter Nine

THE USE OF HUMOR IN COMMUNICATION

When God created me he did not give me athletic ability, intellectual prowess, or any of the other talents that seem to be so highly valued by our society. Yet he did not pass me by. He gave me a gift that will help me live longer and enjoy life more, and it has opened doors to present the gospel to hundreds of thousands of people around the world. He gave me a twisted mind, a sense of humor that causes me to see the world in a different light. There have been times when I have struggled with this gift. The communicator of the gospel must discover the balance that allows humor to be used as an effective tool to enhance rather than distract from the message.

Someone defined humor as "a gentle way to acknowledge human frailty." Put another way, humor is a way of saying, "I'm not okay and you're not okay, but that's okay, he loves us anyway!" Humor is possible only when people are willing to acknowledge their frailty. The same attitude that makes it possible to admit to God that we are imperfect sinners and rejoice in the fact that he loves us in spite of our imperfection makes it possible to laugh at human imperfection and the imperfections in the world around us.

A misguided television evangelist once wrote that anyone who uses humor in the communication of the gospel is not Spirit-led. Humor, he said, is a tool of the devil. On the contrary, the human spirit can laugh from the depths of the soul only when freed from the bondage of sin. Much of today's negative perversion of comedy and humor is inappropriate in its own right, but just because humor has been misused doesn't mean it can't be properly used to glorify God.

This chapter is designed to help you develop humor as a tool in your communication arsenal. It will show why humor is important, what makes something funny, and how you can use this valuable resource in your communication. It also covers ways to know what is appropriate, where to look for humor, and how you can develop this skill to fit your own communication style, personal ability, and ministry situation. Whether you think of yourself as a humorous person or not, whether you believe your audience will be receptive to humor or not, this chapter has some valuable insights for you.

THE VALUE OF HUMOR

Before you would even want to develop the skill of using humor in your communication you would have to be convinced of its value. Humor is important for several reasons.

First of all, *humor benefits the mind and body.*

How did a man who sells ice cream ever get to be called the Good Humor man? He didn't tell jokes. It was because of the reactions he elicited in the faces and hearts of hundreds of children when they heard the music played by the ice cream truck. Little eyes would sparkle and children would wake out of sound sleep to greet the man who drove that truck.

Audiences greet the speaker who effectively uses humor the same way. There is anticipation and excitement that causes the blood to flow and the mind to be more alert. Someone has said that humor is internal jogging. It's just plain good for you. Norman Cousins chronicles the simple health benefits of laughter:

> It worked. I made the joyous discovery that ten minutes of genuine belly laughter had an anesthetic effect and would give me at least two hours of pain-free sleep. When the pain-killing effect of the laughter wore off, we would switch on the motion picture projector again, and, not infrequently, it would lead to another pain-free sleep interval. Sometimes, the nurse read to me out of a trove of humor books. Especially usefully were E. B. and Katharine White's *Subtreasury of American Humor* and Max Eastman's *The Enjoyment of Laughter.*
>
> How scientific was it to believe that laughter—as well as the positive emotions in general—was affecting my body chemistry for the better? If laughter did in fact have a salutary effect on the body's chemistry, it seemed at least theoretically likely that it would enhance the system's ability to fight the inflammation. So we took sedimentation rate readings just before as well as several hours after the laughter episodes. Each time, there was a drop of at least five points. The drop by itself was not substantial, but it held and was cumulative. I was greatly elated by the

discovery that there is a physiological basis for the ancient theory that laughter is good medicine. (*Anatomy of an Illness as Perceived by the Patient: Reflections on Healing and Regeneration* [Norton, 1979], 39)

There have been times when I have struggled over whether or not to use humor in my presentations. Because of the importance of the gospel I am anxious to get right down to business. I've asked myself, "Is there any benefit to making people laugh?"

A church once asked me to come for the sole purpose of making the people laugh. Of course I was free to share the message of the gospel, but they asked me to keep it light. That evening, I spoke to about seven hundred adults at a Valentine banquet held in the church basement. The audience roared with laughter throughout the evening. Even though I shared with that group what the power of God's grace had done in my life, at the end of the evening I felt a little guilty that I didn't get "more heavy."

When I finished an elderly lady, her face still flushed from laughing came up and clutched my hand. "I don't know how to thank you," she said, her eyes brimming with tears. "Three months ago I lost my husband after forty-five years of marriage. Tonight is the first time I have laughed since he died. I thought that life held no joy without him, but tonight you lifted that burden of depression from my soul. You helped me see that in spite of my sorrow Jesus still has a rich life for me to live." With a heartfelt thank you she gave me one of the most rewarding hugs I have ever received.

Minutes later the pastor of the church drew me aside. (I am always a bit leery when this happens.) He told me how the church had been going through difficult conflict as a result of a building program. "This ... this ..." he struggled to find the right word, "... cleansing we experienced tonight is just what we needed." A letter that followed a few weeks later confirmed that the evening had served as a catalyst for some serious prayer, reconciliation, and a new spirit of cooperation among the members of his congregation.

I'm not suggesting that humor is the answer to every problem; however, there are times when humor breaks down the barrier that keeps people from *seeing* the answer. Humor is just plain good for you.

Second, *humor softens the heart.*

In the foreword to my book *How to Speak to Youth...& Keep Them Awake at the Same Time,* Tony Campolo recalled a time when humor broke the stiff-necked spirit of a group of teenagers and opened their hearts to the gospel. After an evening of laughter and inspiration Tony said of this audience he felt had been unreachable the night before:

> The atmosphere of the convention changed. The next morning the young people greeted me with rapt attention. They hung on my every word.... Ken had done more than just entertain, he made the kids want to listen and respond. He set the stage for one of my most positive experiences speaking with young people!

I have lost count of the times I have stood before an audience that was hostile to the message of Christ, only to see their hearts made soft and receptive by the appropriate use of humor. Whether the audience is six or sixty, humor can break down barriers that almost nothing else can.

After I had spoken before several hundred successful businessmen, one man wrote to say,

> I came prepared to be offended by your religious talk. I wouldn't have been there at all but for a friend who coerced me into going. I was so disarmed by the delightful humor that I forgot to be offended. Before I had a chance to put up my armor I was deeply moved by the truth you presented. My friend and I talked all the way home and I prayed to trust Christ for the first time in my life. Thank you for presenting the truth in a way that could reach someone like me.

Third, *humor lets the audience talk back.*

When people laugh or chuckle or just nod their heads in recognition of the funny truth, they are no longer benchwarmers. They have responded. That move from observer to participant plants whatever truth you are communicating deep into the heart. Chances are much greater that they will remember and act upon what you teach.

Fourth, *humor provides instant feedback.*

It is not always easy to tell when you have lost the attention of an adult audience. Teenagers will roll their eyes and begin to play a miniature game of touch football when you have lost their interest, but polite and savvy adults know how to keep looking at you. You can use humor to find out where you stand with them. If your audience laughs, nods, or chuckles, and the humor you used is solidly connected to the truth you are teaching, then you know immediately that they have heard and understood.

Finally, *humor raises the dead.*

Humor also provides an audible and physical break that snaps an audience back to attention. Many of the best speakers use humor at regular intervals in their presentations because they understand its power to bring the wandering mind back to attention even when the audience doesn't seem to respond.

Once, while making a presentation in the Northeast, I found myself speaking to an audience that didn't seem to be present. There was no visible evidence that they heard what I was saying. Some stared out the window. Others just looked in my direction without any expression. I tried my best humor to get them to respond, but except for an occasional chuckle, it seemed I was getting nowhere. I was particularly disturbed by an elderly gentleman who sat in the front row with arms and legs crossed. With the furrow that he kept in his brow it was lucky his eyes didn't cross. His body language indicated that he wasn't about to enjoy any part of this program even if he had to fight it the entire hour. After a very long hour of intense work with little visible response, I finally closed the program.

The man with the furrow in his brow cornered me by the door. "That was the funniest program I ever heard," he said. "I thought I was going to die." It took all of my will power not to respond, "I thought you had already died."

The point of this true illustration is that even when you are not aware of it, humor is bringing people to life. It recharges batteries and gives the audience the attentive capacity to handle more truth.

WHAT MAKES SOMETHING FUNNY?

That's a serious question. If you know what makes something funny, you can use that knowledge to make anything funny. Some books go into explicit, hair-splitting detail about what makes people laugh. This chapter simply looks at the broad principles so that, without a degree in psychology, you can use those principles to bring humor to your presentations.

To Tell the Truth

The most powerful kind of humor is the humor that is born of simple truth. Few people realize that simply pointing out truth can bring laughter. Consider these: the sign in a jewelry store that offers to pierce ears while you wait (You have to wait to get your ears pierced, don't you?) or the one at the summit of a 14,000-foot mountain that warns "Hill." What makes these things humorous is that they exist.

As I write this I am in the commons area of a Christian cruise ship where most of the passengers are sixty-five years old or older. Last night we hit rough weather that tossed the ship so much that you could barely walk down the hall without bumping into the walls on both sides. As I started my talk for the evening I mentioned that I had never seen so many staggering Baptists in all my life. I was totally surprised by the outburst of laughter. A statement of simple truth coupled with its mental image of staggering Baptists brought smiles and laughter from the entire group.

I often point out to parents that we take ourselves far too seriously. When I remind parents of some of the silly things they say, they laugh as they recognize the truth. How many times has a parent cornered a child with the words "You look at me when I'm talking to you!" followed immediately by "Don't you look at me like that!" leaving the child with absolutely no place to direct his or her gaze. I laughed out loud at my own ignorance one day when I cornered my teenage daughter and asked, "Do you think I'm stupid?" I suddenly realized that I didn't want a truthful answer. Judging from the laughter of audiences who hear this story, I am not the only one who has asked that question.

Humor that comes from simple truth is low-risk humor. Even if people don't laugh the truth still remains. If that truth is tied securely to the rationale or objective of your message, its purpose is well served whether the audience caught the humor or not. When I ask students of the Dynamic Communicators Workshop if they have ever heard Bill Cosby tell a joke, almost every hand in the class goes up. But they have never heard Bill Cosby tell a joke because Cosby doesn't tell jokes. He talks about real life. His portrayal of family situations and the remembrance of his childhood are simple recollections of slightly exaggerated truth.

The craziness of bureaucracy is suddenly center stage when the speaker mentions the warning tag on his mattress that threatens five years in prison and a $10,000 fine if it is removed. This kind of humor can be used to point out pride, fear, jealousy, and other imperfections that we often ignore except when we are able to laugh at them.

Ridiculous Exaggeration

This is the kind of humor most often associated with comedy. It is very visual and less cerebral than other types of humor. It is high-risk in nature because it will be obvious to the audience that you are trying to be funny. If it fails, it can be embarrassing and can become a barrier to further communication. This is not the kind of humor for beginners or the faint of heart, and there are situations where this kind of humor is not appropriate.

My dad used to say, "If you're going to make a scene, be seen." Exaggerated humor requires total commitment of mind and body and often must be accompanied by acting, exaggerated facial expression, and unique voice inflections. Sunday morning service, an address at the Rotary Club, or an adult Sunday school class would probably not be enhanced by someone making funny faces or talking in a strange voice to get a laugh. On the other hand it might be just the thing that a youth leader would use to grab the attention of his students. Once again, regardless of the situation this is the kind of humor that must be done well in order to succeed.

Examples of exaggerated humor are most often found with outright comedy. Bill Cosby screws up his face and threatens to run over his son because he brought the car home without filling it with gas. Steven Wright wonders out loud whether some skeletons might have humans hidden in their closets. Robin Williams impersonates a Martian who has just opened a container of L'eggs panty hose. These are all hilarious routines that make full use of exaggeration. They are often limited to performance situations and require exceptional confidence and skill to be effective.

Your own personality and communication situation may eliminate most exaggerated humor from your repertoire. Don't be discouraged by that fact. If you can't sing opera, there are many other kinds of music you can use to express yourself. Similarly, you can find humor that fits your style and situation even if you never use exaggerated comedy-style humor.

Surprise Surprise

The kind of humor most often used in the telling of a joke is humor based on surprise. The punch line is a line that often takes the listener in a direction opposite of the direction the story was leading. It is the clever surprise of this punch line that tickles the funny bone. This kind of humor is also high-risk but does not require the same level of skill that exaggerated humor does. It is acceptable in a wider range of communication situations.

> I broke a mirror the other day and heard I was supposed to get seven years of bad luck. My lawyer thinks he can get me off with three.

> A lady who continually refused to fly because of fear was challenged by her son, "Your refusal to fly shows the weakness of your faith," he exhorted.

"Jesus said that he would be with us always." "No
he didn't," the woman retorted, "He said, *Low*, I am
with you always."

There are many other subtle forms of humor such as special plays on words, unique definitions, etc., but almost
all of them fall into one of the categories listed earlier. It is
also important to note that much humor makes use of a
combination of the elements I've described. If you experience something that you wish to share with your audience you can use the principles already suggested to
make it funny.

*A little boy working on a report for school laid down his pencil
and inquired of his mother. "Mom, where did I come from?"
The mother had intended to talk with her son about this but was
too busy at the moment so she responded, "The stork brought
you." Finding his grandmother in the living room he asked,
"Grandmother, where did I come from?" Grandmother was not
about to broach this subject so she responded. "The stork
brought you just like he brought me and your mother." The boy
went back to his room, picked up his pencil and began his report
with these words: "There hasn't been a normal birth in our family for three generations."*

When I heard this story, I burst out with laughter at the
surprise of the ending. How much less effective this
would have been if the speaker had said, "A boy once
thought that his family had abnormal births because they
told him the stork brought him." This demonstrates the
principle of timing in humor. Arrange the telling of your
story so the surprise is saved until last. Don't give away
the surprise and then expect laughter. Even when using

simple truth for humor, try it out on your friends before you deliver it in public. Learn to tell your story in such a way that it maximizes the principles that will make it funny.

GET SERIOUS ABOUT HUMOR

Following are some considerations important to the communicator who wants to develop humor.

Know your own style and ability

Many are reluctant to try humor because they believe that to be humorous you must be a comedian. However, many excellent communicators who use humor are not naturally funny people. I have come to accept gratefully the fact that God has made me a funny person. Many times people laugh when I say things that I don't even consider funny. I enjoy making people laugh and find it quite easy, but you don't have to have a twisted mind like mine to use humor. The range of humor extends all the way from wit that elicits a knowing nod to comedy that triggers uncontrollable laughter. Somewhere within those boundaries you will find humor that is consistent with your own style and ability.

Whatever you do it is important that you don't try to be someone you are not. If you are not a naturally funny person the humor you use will probably be closer to intellectual wit or poignant anecdote than outright comedy. Some of my favorite humorists are people who would never make it as a stand-up comedian.

Mark Twain had a dry, satirical wit that also conveyed intelligence and wisdom, yet I don't think there were a lot of belly laughs in response to his speeches.

One of my favorites, Will Rogers, elicited laughter yet remained dignified and intelligent in his delivery. "I don't belong to an organized political party," he said, "I'm a Republican!"

Tony Campolo uses a unique and dynamic delivery that is peppered with exaggeration, surprise, and truth. He uses the full range of humor to communicate a message that is very serious.

Even Billy Graham frequently uses humor in his presentation, but you will never hear him use voice inflections, or exaggerated facial expressions, because for him that would be totally out of character. Be yourself.

Don't set yourself up for failure

All humor can be divided into two basic categories: high-risk humor and low-risk humor. High-risk humor is the kind that demands a response of laughter. An obvious joke or exaggerated humor falls into this category.

If you stand in front of an audience and announce, "I heard a good one the other day, you're going to love it," you are attempting high-risk humor. If the audience doesn't laugh at the end of your story, there is going to be an embarrassing silence that comedians call death. It doesn't matter that you don't consider yourself a comedian, if you set your audience up for laughter and don't deliver, you will die just like a comedian.

Even without an introduction some jokes and stories are high-risk. Consider telling a story that begins like this: "One day a man walked into a pet shop and asked if he could buy a Christian parrot." You are already in high-risk territory. The very concept of the story tips your audience that this is supposed to be funny. Now you've got to deliver. When humor fails, it hinders communication and takes a painful slice out of the speakers self-esteem. For that reason I suggest you use low-risk humor to start with. There are two kinds of low-risk humor. The first kind includes jokes and stories that are so good that they never fail. Those kind are few and far between. Test them first and practice your timing before you deliver them in a critical situation. Even a sure-fire story can be ruined with a sloppy delivery.

The second kind of low-risk humor is the best. This type of humor is composed of true stories or other illustrations that carry their own weight even if no one laughs. Humor born of truth falls into this category. These kinds of stories are perfect for developing humorous skills because you have nothing to lose.

Our four-year-old daughter threw her hip against our bedroom door one morning and with indignation announced, "I've had a tooth under my pillow for three days." With her hands firmly planted on her hips, she groused, "If the fairy doesn't come tonight she is going to be missing some teeth of her own." Then she turned on her heel and left the room.

I often use this story to show how we begin early in life to lose patience over little things. Most of the time this story gets laughter, but even when it doesn't nothing is lost. It is low-risk humor, and the story stands on its own as a good illustration. This kind of humor also gives you the opportunity to try it more than once, practicing your timing and delivery until you get it right. Just be sure that you don't deliver your story and then wait for laughter. Doing that immediately turns a low-risk situation into a high-risk situation. If you expect laughter and it doesn't come, just continue without pausing and no one will ever know.

BE AWARE OF THE DOUBLE EDGE OF HUMOR

Humor is like a double-edged sword. One edge can be used to build up and encourage, and the other edge can be used to destroy. You must be very careful to know which edge of the sword you are wielding. It is interesting to watch children use both sides of this sword with skill.

Teenagers will often adopt nicknames for each other derived from some perceived imperfection. A boy with large feet may be called "Shoes" by his buddies. This demonstrates that his friends recognize that he has big feet, but they like him anyway. A boy in my school walked through a plate glass door and from that day forward was affectionately referred to as "Spook" because he had the ability to walk through walls. Yet teenagers use the same type of humor to ostracize and humiliate people they don't like. They know how to use both edges of the sword.

Some people contend that this kind of humor should never be used. I disagree. Among friends it is a way of showing intimacy and acceptance. However, it should never be used with strangers. What you meant to be a gesture of humorous acceptance can easily be taken as a cruel remark by someone you don't know. An audience that is not familiar with you may not take kindly to this kind of humor even if it is directed toward a friend. They have no way of knowing you are friends and simply conclude that you are insensitive and cruel. In this regard ethnic humor is potentially lethal and should be avoided. Although you may have an ethnic friend in the audience with whom you are accustomed to making such exchanges, the chances are slim that the audience will accept such humor even if delivered with the best intentions.

I should caution you that you will not please everybody with your humor. If you use humor you are going to receive some criticism. The key is to know your audience and use humor that is appropriate. If you are unsure whether something is appropriate, it is probably good counsel not to use it. Remember, humor is a tool to enhance your communication. If you feel a story or joke might stand in the way of that communication, don't hesitate to eliminate it from your presentation.

Unfortunately, there are also those who feel that humor has no part in any presentation of the gospel. If you are in a church where that view prevails, or if you find yourself in a situation where the audience would be offended if you used humor, deliver your speech with power and dignity and move on. In fifteen years of ministry in which I have used humor extensively, I have run into few people who are totally humorless and few churches that won't accept some humor even in worship.

Usually it's the style of delivery that determines whether it is appropriate or not. There are stories I use in concert where I jump all over the stage, contort my face, and use strange accents. When I tell the same stories in a worship service, I do it without all the accompanying body English and it's perfectly acceptable.

Watch other people

Develop the eye of the hunter as you look for humor in everyday situations and watch and learn from people who are experts at humor. Listen to how Bill Cosby gets people to laugh by telling a story about something that most people have experienced. Stand-up comedians are not so valuable a resource as communicators who use humor well. Howard Hendricks and Tony Campolo are a couple of examples. Watch these people and see how they make their delivery. Be aware of the timing that can make or break humor and watch how the audience responds to different attempts at humor. When you see humor fail, ask yourself why and try to analyze how it might have been done differently.

Practice, practice, practice

Use friends, a spouse, or anyone who is friendly enough to listen. Begin to work low-risk humor into your presentations and don't be discouraged with occasional failure. This entire chapter is devoted to humor because it is a powerful tool and well worth developing.

Recall the definition of humor attributed to Victor Borge: "The shortest distance between two people." That puts it in a nutshell. We have the greatest message in the universe and any legitimate method of opening hearts to receive that message should be explored to the fullest.

Chapter Ten

BODY LANGUAGE

Appearances can be deceiving. How many times have you judged someone on the basis of outward appearance only to discover you were wrong? A sloppily dressed person may surprise you with the delivery of a well-organized, persuasive speech. But first you must overcome the barrier of that first impression. Likewise the importance of a well-prepared speech may be lost if the communicator delivers that speech without passion or expression. Body language, facial expression, and gestures convey the conviction that makes you believable. This chapter deals with how you can use your body to enhance the power of your communication.

BE AWARE OF YOUR APPEARANCE

Why should those of us who communicate the message of the gospel be concerned about how we look? Because the audience we are trying to reach is very much affected by outward appearance. Sloppy dress, outdated styles, and poor choice of clothing can distract and cause the audience to prejudge the value of what you are about to say. As much as I try to concentrate on the content of the speech, I even find myself distracted by careless dressing.

Here are some principles that may keep you from hindering your communication efforts.

1. Be stylish, but don't overdo it.

It is always a good rule to dress slightly more formally than the audience. Although some may come to church dressed in jeans and sweatshirts, it enhances the image of the pastor, teacher, or youth leader to be "dressed up." This doesn't mean the speaker has to wear a designer suit or dress, it simply means that your appearance should convey the idea that you are to be taken seriously.

In many ways vestments, which some ministers wear, solve this problem. Clerical garb not only symbolizes authority, it also nullifies the tendency to criticize style. If the pastor is wearing such a garment no one is going to be distracted by the loudness of his tie, the cut of her dress, or the specific label of the garment.

But many pastors don't wear vestments. The communication efforts of youth workers and Sunday school teachers would be hindered by such a garment. Still, your goal in dress ought to accomplish the same end. You should strive to be stylish enough not to distract by being old-fashioned, and conservative enough not to distract by being flamboyant. As a communicator you are trying to make a *statement*, but usually not a *fashion* statement.

Your audience should determine how you will dress. When speaking to the corporate executives of IBM, dress accordingly. When speaking to youth, be careful not to be too formal. I worked with youth for many years and became fully aware of their obsession with style and dress. I'm sure they would be distracted if at camp I got up to speak in a three-piece business suit. As a teenager, however, I was always distracted by the other extreme: the speaker who presented his message dressed in shorts and a sloppy T-shirt. The knees of anyone over thirty are not usually a pretty sight. Teenagers don't expect adults to dress exactly like them to be accepted, but they will expect you to be up-to-date.

Not only is it important to wear the appropriate clothing, but it is also important to know how to wear it. I am always distracted watching a man try to communicate a serious and intelligent message with a tie that reaches only halfway to his belt. This is especially bad if the skinny part of the tie is hanging two inches below the wide part. Many people would have a difficult time taking seriously a person with this appearance.

I used to laugh at the concept of color coordination until I was made to realize that we live in a society that is very aware of poor color combinations. On more than one occasion I have given thanks for a wife who sent me back to the closet to take off the green tie because it didn't go with the navy suit.

Here are some simple rules:

- Always try to dress slightly more formally than your audience.

- Know how to combine colors and the proper way to wear clothes.

- When traveling bring clothes that will give you flexibility. Nothing is more uncomfortable than to arrive at an informal gathering in formal clothes or vice versa.

- When in doubt lean toward the conservative.

- Seek the advice of those who know.

2. Keep clean and well groomed

Recently I received a videotape of a speech I had given in front of 11,000 teenagers. I heard my children chuckling as they watched the tape. I was mortified to see that I had given that entire speech looking like Dennis the Menace. Several hairs on the back of my head were sticking straight up in the air. Not only did it show up on the small television, but at the actual event my image had been projected larger than life on a thirty-foot screen. Those few hairs must have looked like palm trees swaying in the breeze. No one walked out of the meeting because of those hairs, but I am sure that they were a distraction. Well-kept hair, freshly ironed clothes, clean fingernails, shined shoes, and fresh breath are all an important part of a professional appearance.

3. Do a last-minute check

Few speakers approach the microphone intending to look disheveled and unkempt, but unless you do a last-minute check you could easily give an impassioned speech with one side of your collar sticking straight up. On three separate occasions I have tried to communicate to an audience who would not listen because I had neglected to check my fly. (I have talked with dozens of other speakers who have made the same mistake.) I watched in amaze-

Would you buy a philosophy from this man?

ment one night as a woman gave an entire speech with an earring caught in her hair. Through the entire speech, it hung just below her jaw, suspended by an invisible thread of hair.

Before you move to the front of any room to do any kind of communication make a last-minute check of your hair, tie, buttons, zippers, shirt tail, and accessories.

ESTABLISH GOOD EYE CONTACT

"Look at me when I'm speaking to you." How many times a parent has used those words to establish eye contact with a child. The most well-prepared speech delivered with poor eye contact will lose much of its effectiveness. It is the eyes that convey sincerity and conviction. All the passion you can muster in the tone of your voice as you proclaim, "I love you," will not register if you don't look into the eyes of the one you say you love. Parents insist that children look into their eyes to see whether they are telling the truth. Few people will buy a used car from a salesperson with shifty eyes. If a person won't look at you, you feel he can't be trusted. Lack of good eye contact will be interpreted by your audience as a lack of confidence, insincerity, apathy, or outright deception. Recognize and avoid the bad habits associated with poor eye contact.

DON'T BE A SWEEPER

One of the most common bad habits among speakers is the practice of sweeping the audience without ever focusing on any one person. An audience is simply a group of individuals. If you neglect to recognize those individuals by never establishing personal eye contact, your whole audience will feel left out. Even though you may not look at every person, your presentation will be much more personal if you establish eye contact with individuals. Don't be a sweeper.

DON'T BE A SHIFTER

A shifter can establish individual eye contact, but only for a brief moment. This undesirable habit will cause your audience to think that you are ashamed or have something to hide. Shifty eyes have always been associated with someone who can't be trusted. As one who is entrusted with the most important message on earth, you don't want to be misread in this way. Don't be a shifter.

DON'T BE A BIRD WATCHER

The speaker with the bird-watcher habit occasionally acknowledges the audience with a glance or two but spends much of the time looking at other items of interest. The bird watcher gazes out the window, examines flaws in the woodwork, or finds any other safe haven that will keep him or her from seeing real people. I once watched a man give an entire message watching a spider crawl across the ceiling. Instead of being focused on the speaker, most of the eyes in the room were on the spider.

Nothing other than people in your audience should capture your attention. Professional stage entertainers are taught early in their careers not to be distracted by backstage sound. Don't be a bird watcher.

DON'T BE A DREAMER

The dreamer is the speaker who gazes into empty space during the presentation of the message. The eyes are focused on nothing. Unfortunately, the audience listening to a dreamer will often conclude that there is also nothing between this speaker's ears. The most intelligent presentation delivered by a speaker who seems to be in another world will not be received with the respect it deserves. Don't be a dreamer.

DON'T BE A READER

The reader finds sanctuary from personal eye contact by keeping his head buried in a script. Although a motivated audience might survive such a delivery, most audiences will quickly lose interest. Even if you prepare scripted messages it is important to be familiar enough with that message to be able to look up and acknowledge your audience. If you intend to read a speech it would save much time and effort simply to put it on tape. Don't be a reader. Establish the habits of good eye contact.

SPEAK TO INDIVIDUALS

An audience is made up of individuals who want to be acknowledged. One evening I watched a speaker get up and spend about thirty seconds looking around the audience, making eye contact with many of the people there. Occasionally he would nod or smile as someone acknowledged the eye contact. Just as I began to wonder if he was ever going to speak, the man took a deep breath and said, "I can see that I am going to enjoy the next half hour." Wow, what a way to win an audience. Basically he was saying, "I see you and I like you." Even those who had not been directly affected by his kind gaze felt that he was aware of their presence.

As you speak, pick out individuals in the audience and speak directly to them, make sure that you include those who sit farther back and at the edges of your audience.

COMPLETE A THOUGHT WITH ONE PERSON

In a society that craves intimacy and fears it at the same time, eye contact can be a little uncomfortable. I used to tell my students that they should "look until it hurts." In other words, they should keep the eye contact with a single individual until it begins to feel uncomfortable. Unfortunately it got uncomfortable so quickly, that they changed from dreamers and sweepers into shifters. They would establish eye contact and then immediately look away. Since then I have asked students to complete a thought while keeping eye contact with one person and then move on to establish contact with someone else.

I am always asked whether eye contact won't make the audience uncomfortable and turn them off. I can't remember ever seeing someone establish such intense eye contact that it negatively affected communication, but I have seen hundreds who seemed to communicate a lack of confidence and even shame by their refusal to acknowledge the individuals in the audience with sustained eye contact.

KNOW HOW TO HANDLE LARGE AUDIENCES

In a large audience it is still important to practice the principles of good eye contact. Even when you cannot make out the faces of those in the back of the auditorium, pick out one person and complete a thought with that person. Imagine that it is just you and she in a conversation, and communicate your thought with sincerity and personal conviction. If you speak to no one, no one will think you are speaking to him or her. On the other hand, it has been proved that if you pick out someone far back in the audience and speak directly to that person, many seated near that person will believe that you are speaking to them.

Many times I find myself speaking in situations where I can see absolutely nothing. The auditorium lights have been dimmed and two or three spotlights render me legally blind. I used to struggle in these situations until a kind pastor who was actually close to legally blind shared a secret. "I can't see a thing beyond my notes," he confided, "but I know most of the families that are out there. Although I can't see who the people are I direct my message to specific members of my congregation. I may not be looking at Mr. Smith, but in my mind I'm talking to him personally. Then I talk to little Jenny Horton awhile. In this way my audience is never aware that I can't see who they are."

This man in his seventies is one of the finest communicators I have ever met. Even though he can't see, he talks to individual people. Eye contact is a very important ingredient in dynamic communication.

REMOVE YOUR GLASSES WHEN YOU SPEAK

If at all possible, remove your glasses when you speak. Most of the time the light reflecting from the lens of a pair of glasses will completely obliterate any glimpse of the speaker's eyes. Most communications courses make this recommendation, yet only a few speakers follow the advice.

If you use a manuscript and your eyesight is so bad that you can't read without your glasses, then it may be more of a hindrance to do without them, but with a little practice most speakers find it quite simple to put their glasses on when they need to read and remove them when they are speaking. Let the audience get the full benefit of good eye contact.

PRACTICE UNTIL GOOD EYE CONTACT IS NATURAL

Developing the habit of good eye contact does not come easily. It takes a lot of practice. Have friends or your spouse constantly critique your eye contact. Describe a dreamer, shifter, and sweeper and ask them to point out when you slip into those bad habits. My wife reminds me when I slip into the habit of speaking to only one side of the room. I have excellent eye contact; it's just that I tend to discriminate and give it to only half the audience. I treat the audience on the right side of the room as though they don't exist, and it is only with her help that I become aware of it.

You can also practice with a video camera. Place the camera somewhere in the audience and as you speak make a conscious effort to use good eye contact. Include the camera. That's right! Several times make an effort to look into the lens and complete a thought. When you watch this video you will immediately spot any tendency to shift or sweep, and you will be amazed at the power of eye contact when your own gaze comes to rest on you. You might even get convicted by your own message. The video camera is a powerful tool for growing in excellence as a communicator. Use it often to check up on your eye contact.

Daily conversation provides another opportunity for practice. Look at people as you converse with them. Don't just look in their direction, look into their eyes. You will find it easier to practice the same kind of eye contact with large groups.

LET YOUR BODY LANGUAGE MATCH YOUR WORDS

Have you ever watched a speaker talk about the joy of living for Christ with an expression that seemed more appropriate for attending the funeral of a favorite pet?

Body Language

When someone says, "Boy, was that speaker enthusiastic!" he is not describing the words but the facial expressions, the body language, and the tone of voice that accompanied the words.

It is the face that makes the audience believe that you believe what you say. When you really believe what you say, your whole body gets involved. Can you picture a woman walking slowly down the corridor of her apartment building repeating quietly, in a monotone voice, "Fire. Fire. Help. The building is on fire." Of course not. If such a scene should occur, I doubt that anyone would pay attention. But such a scene would never happen. A woman with that kind of urgent message would be wide-eyed, waving her arms, and screaming at the top of her lungs, "FIRE! FIRE!"

When you speak of joy, does your face show it? Can people see in your body language those things that make you sad? Does your expression leave no doubt that you are excited about the Christianity you proclaim?

One student responded to that question by saying, "Oh, I can do that. I took drama classes for three years in college." He missed the point. There is no need to act. Simply allow your whole body to communicate. Of all people, communicators ought to be the ones who wear their hearts on their sleeves. Of course, it is possible to get too emotional and hinder your communication, but in all my years of teaching I have seen only a few who carry body language to the extreme. Most don't even begin to tap the potential of this aspect of communication.

Before you give your next sermon or talk, deliver it into a mirror or video camera. Ask yourself, "If I were listening to this person, would I think that he or she was excited about what is being said? Would the enthusiasm make me want to hear more?"

Ask, "How would I express myself if I were sharing this truth with a close friend?" If messages were delivered with half the excitement we use in everyday conversation, audience interest would pick up dramatically.

USE APPROPRIATE GESTURES

The same advise given above applies to gestures. We walk around all day waving our arms and making extensive use of our hands as we communicate to everyone around us. But when we step up to speak it's as though the arms are hollow and someone has poured them full of cement. Or in front of an audience we repeat one gesture over and over like a robot with a short circuit. Nervous tension and habit are the culprits. Relax and carry your gestures to their fullest extent.

Tension turns even experienced speakers into flippers. Flippers let their arms hang like lead at their sides, and all their gestures are reduced to a little helpless flipping motion of the hands. It doesn't matter whether the speaker is describing a tiny breath of wind or a major hurricane, the same anemic flip of the wrist is used to describe both. Others interlock their fingers at about waist level just to make sure those hands don't get out of control.

Free yourself up! Let your hands paint the pictures your lips describe.

Just as it is nearly impossible to have too much eye contact, so it is almost impossible to overdo gestures. Occasionally I run across a flapper (one whose gestures are so exaggerated that they detract from the message), but it is extremely rare. Practice with the mirror, videotaping, and constructive critique from friends. If you think of your speech as a conversation with a friend, it will help you relax. The only difference between talking with a friend and talking to a group is the number of friends in the room.

Enlist others to help you identify those habitual gestures and quirky motions that detract from communication. It was only after repeated suggestions from my wife that I took the time to watch a video to see one of these gremlins in my own presentation. Out of habit I would constantly pinch my nose. In one speech alone I reached up and grabbed my nose twenty-one times. This unneeded gesture did nothing to enhance my talk, and I was totally unaware that I was doing it.

At an Easter service I heard one of the finest messages on the Resurrection ever presented. Unfortunately the pastor had a distracting habit that no one had ever been kind enough to bring to his attention. As he began a dramatic phrase he would pull his head down until it looked as though he had no neck. Then as he delivered the phrase he would increase in volume and slowly, with a jerky mechanical kind of motion extend his neck to its maximum length. After the service we were invited to attend a luncheon along with other visitors to the church. The conversation in several groups centered not around the excellent content of the pastor's message, but the unique turtle-like quality of the pastor's neck.

Very seldom will you find someone in your audience willing to risk telling you that you look like a turtle. So it is of utmost importance that you use video and the critique of friends to spot those distracting motions and exorcise them from your presentations.

STAND AND DELIVER

One very important aspect of your communication is the way you stand. I have watched communicators of every age, sex, and ability sway rhythmically as they speak, causing seasickness in a significant proportion of the audience. I have watched as they paced like a caged lion or simply walked in small circles like a bewildered beast. I've seen speakers draped on the podium like a lion in the afternoon sun or watched as a person shifted weight from one foot to another with a frequency that caused me to worry if the hip joint would hold. I personally have become rooted on one side of the platform to deliver the entire speech to one side of the audience. Most of these tendencies can be corrected by practicing correct posture and stance.

To communicate with authority and confidence, stand with your feet slightly apart and one foot slightly ahead of the other. With your weight evenly distributed between both feet, bend slightly at the waist and lean toward the audience. Communicate a complete thought using this confident stance, then if you are going to move, do it between thoughts. When you move, move with purpose. Do it only to emphasize your next point with a different segment of the audience. Random pacing is very distracting. Get where you want to be, take a solid stand, and communicate again.

Stand on your own two feet. Avoid leaning against podiums, pulpits, music stands, or other solid objects.

In conclusion, the object is not to become an actor or entertainer who plays with people's emotions, but to allow your body to express the concepts and emotions you are teaching with your lips. When communicating the Good News of Jesus Christ don't be afraid to let your body talk.

Chapter Eleven

CONTROLLING YOUR ENVIRONMENT TO ENHANCE COMMUNICATION

While visiting a church not long ago I found myself strangely depressed. The music was excellent and the pastor's message was well-prepared and to the point, yet I couldn't shake a dreary feeling. About halfway through the service I realized the cause of it. I couldn't see anything. The dark stained-glass windows held out much of the light, and the available light in the church threw foreboding shadows over the eyes of all who ventured near the front. To make matters worse, the sound system gave the pastor's voice a tinny quality and rang with an annoying squeal whenever his voice hit a certain tone. This sincere man of God was trying to communicate a message of love and hope in a depressing environment.

Your environment profoundly influences the effectiveness of your communication. This chapter will cover the steps you can take to control your environment to enhance the effectiveness of your communication.

LET THERE BE LIGHT

One of the first things that God did after he created the earth was to command, "Let there be light." Ever since that day he has chosen to work in the light, he refers to himself as light, and he created a people that prefers light to darkness unless they are seeking to do evil (John 3:19). Why then are the buildings we call his house so often dark and dingy?

Lighting sets the atmosphere of a room. As far as I'm concerned, the atmosphere of a monastery is not conducive to twentieth-century worship. The church service I mentioned earlier was rendered impersonal and cold by the faceless bodies that spoke from the podium. Furthermore, the faces were made downright spooky by the inadequate lighting coming from above.

If you want to set a temporary mood of dreary darkness, have a lighting system that will adjust to that level at *the appropriate time*, but the sermon is *not* the appropriate time.

When the communicator's face is visible, the communication is much more powerful. When the communicator's eyes are visible the communication is a hundredfold more powerful than that.

Many people have become so accustomed to poor lighting that they are unaware of its negative effect. But it does have an effect.

I was once asked to speak at a gathering of about eight hundred people in Canada. When I arrived I discovered that the lighting was terrible. The meeting was held in a huge gymnasium, and the only light came from dim incandescent bulbs high in the ceiling. As one of the organizers of the event walked across the stage I could see none of the features in his face. I couldn't tell whether he was smiling or frowning or whether he had been born without a face. I was standing in about the third row at the time, so you can imagine what the people in the back could see.

I make maximum use of facial expression in my speaking, yet I was being asked to communicate in darkness. I begged the man to find some way to light that stage. I had kindly requested adequate lighting months before coming, but those requests had been ignored. Because they had never used additional lighting in the past, they saw no reason to start now. I could tell that my host was a little angry about my concern even though I explained that my only desire was to create an environment in which to communicate effectively. After some scrambling he located a light used for a home movie camera and improvised a stand to hold it. It was far from perfect, but the harsh light provided just enough illumination so everyone could see my face.

For the first fifteen minutes of the speech, the audience responded with enthusiasm and spirit. Then suddenly the light went out, leaving only the dim ceiling lights. I continued my presentation, but the spirit of the audience changed immediately. The audience laughter seemed forced and died away as quickly as it had begun. I rarely have trouble controlling a group, but within minutes I could hear some of the young people in the back begin to have their own conversations. After several minutes someone discovered the plug had been kicked from the wall and plugged it back in. When the light came back on

there was spontaneous applause from the audience. The attention of the kids in the back snapped back to the stage, and the group responded with the same delighted enthusiasm that they exhibited at the beginning of the program.

The audience would never have been conscious of the lack of light had they not been able to see clearly in the first part of the program, but its absence would have affected their attitudes and responses throughout the entire program. The host apologized profusely after the program. "I never realized," he said, "the difference that good lighting makes."

Christianity is about new life in Christ. Does the place that you present this wonderful message look like a place to celebrate life or is it more like a morgue?

Here is a test you can conduct to see whether the lighting in your situation is adequate for good communication. Have someone stand where you usually stand when you speak, then walk to the back of the room or auditorium. If from the back you can see all the facial features of the person in front clearly, give yourself a C+. If there are no shadows in the eye sockets or under the nose give yourself a B+. Lighting that is too close to the front and coming from too sharp an angle will create these hideous shadows. They make the eyes look hollow and sunken, and give the speaker the appearance of a talking skull. If you can see a pinpoint of reflected light in the eyes of the person up front give yourself an A+.

That is the kind of lighting that is most conducive to good communication. That kind of lighting makes a room feel warm and interesting and has a way of brightening the spirit. If you take out a recent professional photograph of yourself or a friend you will see that pinpoint of light in the eye. It is so important to bringing life to the photo that if it does not appear in the original print the photographer will touch up the photo and paint it in. In larger auditoriums you won't see this pinpoint of light from the back, but if the lighting is right, it should be visible from closer up.

They say that the eyes are the window to the soul. The eyes are the first place to see indications that your children are sick or that they are lying. The sincerity and integrity that can be communicated only with the eyes will be lost on the audience if they can't see the eyes. Time after time I have seen poor lighting draw power from an excellent message. I have given substantial space to this subject because of the important role this overlooked factor has on communication.

For small groups such as Sunday school classes and Bible studies, the lighting is not so critical because the teacher or speaker is close enough to be seen. Even so, make sure these rooms are bright and cheery. For larger youth groups and Sunday school classes (fifty or more) some kind of additional lighting will usually be beneficial. If the room is relatively small, this can be done inexpensively. Light these rooms so that you can clearly see facial expressions and the pinpoint of light in the eye.

Figure 1

OBJECTIONS TO GOOD LIGHTING

Although lighting a church sanctuary properly need not be expensive, it is often difficult to get a church body to agree to purchase the necessary equipment. Here are some common objections.

The light gets in our eyes.

This objection will be raised by those who speak from the platform. The truth is that good lighting will always be in the eyes of the speaker. Good lighting is a little uncomfortable for the speaker, especially at first. Eventually you get used to it and forget it is even there. But be prepared—the budget committee chairman will never get used to it.

It focuses attention on the pastor instead of the Lord.

I have never understood this kind of thinking, but it comes up all the time. Carried to its conclusion, this argument would require the pastor to be out of sight completely to give his message. It is the pastor's calling to proclaim the gospel to those in the congregation. To do that effectively, he must be visible. Once he is seen it is his responsibility to focus the attention on Jesus. If the communicator of the gospel is in the dark, I can't guarantee where the attention of the audience will be, but I bet it won't be on the message.

We've done without it for fifty years. There is no need to change now.

Unfortunately this is one objection that is hard to overcome. The best solution I have found is to let the congregation experience the right kind of lighting for several Sundays. Then in the middle of the sermon have someone kick out the plug. You will have a new lighting system within a matter of weeks.

If you decide to enhance the quality of your speaking environment, contact lighting specialists and stay with them during the planning and installation to make sure the guidelines in this chapter are met. In most churches you can buy and install the lights yourself at significantly reduced cost. Once again you can do this effectively if you follow the guidelines. Here they are in simple review.

1. Facial expression should be clearly visible from anywhere in the audience.

2. The lights should be at a low enough angle to avoid casting shadows over the eyes. You can determine this by turning all the other lights off when you do the test. Lower the angle of the lights until the shadows are gone and stop at that point. The glare in the eyes of the speaker will be at a minimum. See Figure 1.

3. Look for the pinpoint of light in the pupil of the speaker's eye. That pinpoint is a primary indication that the lights are at a low enough angle and bright enough. Remember that in larger auditoriums not everyone in the audience will be able to see that pinpoint, but those sitting toward the front should be able to. Two lights can be mounted at an angle off to the side as long as they still create the pinpoint of light and are equal in intensity. Sometime this reduces the glare in the speaker's eyes and allows the lights to be placed at a lower angle. See Figure 2.

197

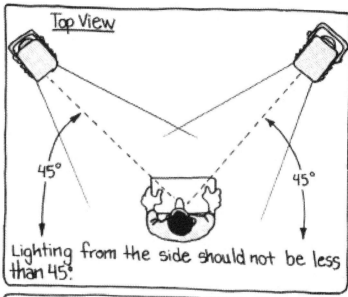

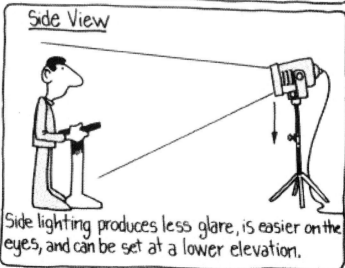

Figure 2

4. Make the light as unobtrusive as possible.

You don't want the front of the church to look like a night club stage. Use soft, unfocused light and flesh-tone gels to get the warm, well-lit effect that doesn't distract.

LET THOSE WHO WILL HEAR, HEAR

Know the importance of good quality sound.

Almost as bad and just as common as poor lighting is a cheap sound system that detracts from the message with its poor quality reproduction and constant squealing feedback.

For three reasons a sound system is important for groups of more than one hundred. First, it enables everyone in the audience to hear clearly. Second, it saves strain on the speaker's voice. Third, it gives the speaker tremendous versatility in voice inflection. With a good sound system even a whisper can be heard.

Know how to recognize good quality sound.

As with lighting, there are methods to determine whether you have or need a good quality sound system. The need for a sound system is as dependent on the acoustics of a room as it is on the size. Some rooms resonate sound well enough so that you can talk in a normal voice and be easily heard by a hundred people. Other rooms soak up sound like a sponge and need a sound system for any size group. Still others reverberate sound, making anything the speaker says unintelligible.

If you can speak softly and the entire audience can still hear what you say with ease, you probably don't need a sound system. If not, then some kind of system would be helpful.

If the system you have sounds tinny and thin, if it tends to give off feedback or a hollow-barrel kind of ringing when the speaker hits certain tones, then you would do well to consider getting something that helps rather than hinders your communication efforts. Test out several systems and look for one that has adjustable equalization (or tone control) so that you can get rid of feedback in a variety of situations. Look for a system that reproduces sound with a rich quality that doesn't make the hair stand up on the back of your neck. If you feel inadequate to make these judgments, find someone who knows about the quality sound systems that music groups use and will be able to tell you what works and what doesn't. Don't rely on the word of a salesperson.

It is also important to remember that a good system is useless unless it has a quality microphone. In almost all church situations it should be omnidirectional and capable of picking up sound from a foot or two away without diminishing its quality. With an omnidirectional microphone you don't have to be exactly in front of the microphone for it to be effective. Get the opinion of someone who knows good sound and will not benefit personally from your purchase.

I recently did a presentation in a new multi-million-dollar facility that had dozens of tiny speakers recessed in the ceiling. Most of them rattled and the feedback problems were tremendous. When I heard what that system cost I almost fell over. For less than half the money this church could have had the best of sound. Make sure you have what you want before you invest. A small church may wish to have portable speakers that can be used in a variety of situations. I have even seen larger churches use such systems economically.

Know how to use the microphone.

1. If the microphone is attached to the podium make sure that it extends far enough back toward the speaker to be useful. Microphones work their best when they are within a few inches of your lips. At first this is uncomfortable, but after awhile you won't even know it is there.

2. Ideally the microphone should be located at a forty-five degree angle just below the lips. If you position the microphone parallel to the floor and at lip height you will get a popping sound every time you pronounce hard consonants like "p."

3. If the microphone is attached to the podium or pulpit, don't allow your hands, books, or papers to hit the podium. Microphones magnify such sounds into loud booms. As a precaution, cushion the microphone holder to minimize this tendency.

4. When you speak into a microphone that is attached to a stand, don't touch the stand or keep removing the microphone. This makes an unbearable noise that is impossible to ignore. If you must remove the microphone, stop speaking, remove it as carefully as possible,

and then continue speaking. In the same vein, *never* adjust a gooseneck microphone holder without first removing the microphone. If you adjust it while it is still in the stand the resulting sound is not unlike the sound of a garbage truck compacting trash.

5. Do not fondle the microphone or its stand. This distracting habit is common among singers and entertainers. It should never be the practice of an effective communicator.

6. Stay close to the microphone. Speakers who are not used to using a microphone often act as if it is electrified. You should never be more than a few inches from it.

7. Adjust the sound levels and height of the microphone before you begin speaking and then *leave it alone.* Chances are that you will remain the same height throughout the speech. Do not allow someone to keep adjusting the volume levels as you speak. These well-meaning people nullify the value of a microphone by trying to keep the volume the same level throughout the speech. One of the assets of the microphone is that it allows you to work with a wide variety of volumes. Learn to use the microphone to your advantage.

The audience isn't even aware of the microphone when it's used properly. Improperly used, it is a distraction that inhibits communication.

ONE SIZE DOESN'T FIT ALL

Match the room to the size of the audience.

When you're trying to set up a good environment for communication, one of the most important rules to remember is to match the size of the room to the size of the audience. This is easier to do for a Sunday school class or youth group than for a small congregation in a big sanctuary.

I was teaching a Sunday school class of about twelve teenagers in a sanctuary that seated about five hundred. In fact, we shared that sanctuary with an adult class about the same size. Our group gathered in the front two pews, and the other class used the back. Not only was it a difficult seating arrangement, but each class could easily hear the teacher of the other class. This is about the worst kind of situation for communication.

Sunday school time is one of the most important learning opportunities in the life of a Christian. Unfortunately it is often treated as a tacked on, second-rate part of church. Give your Sunday school classes and youth groups the environment they deserve.

We solved the problem of two classes in the sanctuary by converting a room that had been used to store banquet tables to accommodate the class. The kids helped me brighten the room with paint and additional lighting. They called the room "the happy dungeon," and the attention level of those kids increased dramatically when we began to meet there.

Another time I taught a small class of adults that was moved from the sanctuary to the living room of a nearby home. Again, the difference in the atmosphere affected the attitude of the group. There is nothing wrong with a sanctuary. But there is something about a small group meeting in such a large place that sets a mood that is not conducive to good communication.

What do you do when the congregation is small, and there is a large sanctuary? You certainly can't move them to the "happy dungeon" or a nearby living room. The answer lies in creating a feeling of community and giving your communication efforts a chance by having the group sit together near the front. A small audience in a large auditorium tends to spread out, leaving the front pews empty. If they sit together near the front, they will be much more receptive then if they are isolated and far from you. It also creates a feeling of community. Be prepared, because some will resist this move. But once they have tasted the warmth of such an arrangement they will not want to go back.

A church in Florida did an experiment with their youth. For three Sundays the entire youth department sat in the front rows of the church during worship. After the third week, even though they were no longer required to do so, the youth stayed in front. They had found the service so much more interesting that they weren't about to give up their seats. The pastor told me that his next project was to get the adults to move up.

Another pastor moved the pulpit halfway down the aisle when the congregation refused to move forward. When people are spread out all over an auditorium, it communicates a coldness that affects the attitude of the audience. Let your congregation know your motivation and get them together and close to you.

LOOK OUT BEHIND YOU

Just as it is important to be seen if you are going to communicate, it is also important not to have other scenes distract from your message as you speak. I have been in beautiful churches that have glass fronts that display breathtaking scenery behind the pastor. To this day I can remember the scenery, but I can't remember anything about the message. Very few churches make the pastor compete with background scenery like this, but if your church is in this situation, lighting can help save the day. Use bright lights so the speaker can be clearly seen against the background.

I remember a discipleship class where the teacher chose to stand in front of a large window whose bottom was at ground level. I spent the entire class trying to tear my attention from a cat that was ambushing every small animal that ventured near. I wanted to listen to the teacher but the visual distraction was just too much.

At a camp in Alaska the speaker chose to stand with his back to a large picture window that looked out on a beautiful snow-covered landscape. Not only was the scenery distracting, but the brightness of the background rendered the speaker only a dark silhouette. I could hardly look toward the front because the brightness hurt my eyes.

It takes only a little planning to avoid these environmental hindrances to communication.

The Alaskan camp speaker moved to the other end of the room where we could see his face, which was illuminated by the natural light coming through the window. And we could look in his direction without going blind. When I first suggested this change, people were reluctant to try it. It would take too much work to rearrange things, they said. (It took less than two minutes.) When the speaker experienced the difference in audience attention he thanked me profusely for the suggestion.

The discipleship class in the basement of the church could have been much more effective if the speaker had recognized that he couldn't compete with a hungry cat and had stood against a different wall. It would have taken only thirty seconds for us to scoot our chairs around.

Here are some simple rules for watching what is behind you.

1. Don't ever stand in front of a window to communicate. The back lighting will make your face only a shadow, it will be uncomfortable for the audience to look in your direction, and you can't compete with scenery.

2. Avoid busy, brightly colored backgrounds. If your church has adjustable lighting, dim the lights on everything that is behind you before you speak.

3. Avoid having anything behind you that moves while you speak. Pastors, if at all possible, dismiss the choir before you begin your message. If you can't dismiss the choir, instruct them to remain as still as possible with their attention fixed on you. I find myself constantly distracted if the choir remains behind the pastor as he speaks. It is particularly difficult if they talk to each other or allow their attention to be drawn away from the preacher.

4. For Sunday school and youth groups, look at the room and ask, "What mood does this room put me in?" Sometimes just a coat of paint can change a dingy, depressing environment into a cheery warm one.

5. Eliminate intrusions into your communication environment. Consider as precious every minute you've allotted for teaching Sunday school, holding a youth meeting, or preaching a sermon. Don't let distractions like taking attendance or the offering interrupt. Arrange to have these activities take place at other times so that you are free to communicate without interruptions. In the best of circumstances communication is a difficult task requiring the best efforts of the speaker. Make sure that your environment is a help and not a hindrance.

Chapter Twelve

BEYOND TECHNIQUE—QUALITIES OF AN EFFECTIVE COMMUNICATOR

In writing a book about the *techniques* of effective communication, I run the risk that someone might infer that *technique alone* can make a good communicator. Clearly, technique can make a difference. In fact, in many cases, it is the single most important factor in making a communicator effective. Still, there is more to communicating than just technique.

An entertaining after-dinner speaker can enhance his presentation by applying proper techniques. So can speakers presenting the gospel. But technique alone will not make a gospel message successful. That doesn't mean that we shouldn't work at perfecting our methods. It means only that we should make sure we establish a proper foundation upon which to build.

If I didn't feel that there is a great need for more excellent presentations of the gospel, I certainly would not have endured the agony of writing a book on the subject. However, in this chapter I would like to discuss issues beyond technique that are important for every messenger of the gospel to consider.

Aristotle said that a good leader must have *logos, ethos,* and *pathos. Logos* is the ability to give solid reasons for an action, to move people intellectually. *Ethos* is the moral character at the source of a leader's ability to persuade. *Pathos* is a leader's ability to touch feelings, to move people emotionally. These same elements must be present in the life of an effective communicator.

THE EFFECTIVE COMMUNICATOR DELIVERS A FOCUSED AND ORGANIZED MESSAGE

If you apply the principles of SCORRE described in the first part of this book, you will have satisfied the *logos* requirement. They provide the organizational and logical foundation for a message that makes sense and has a sharp focus.

But *logos* is not enough. Every day thousands of charlatans and unethical communicators present powerfully focused, organized messages that lead many astray using those same sound communications principles.

If your concern is to communicate, with excellence, the life-changing message of Christ's love, you must attain a higher standard. You must also have *ethos* and *pathos*.

THE EFFECTIVE COMMUNICATOR MODELS THE MESSAGE

No matter what kind of audience you have—whether it be a Bible study group, a congregation, a youth group, or a Sunday school class—you will influence your audience as much by your life as by your message. In fact, your life will provide a strong foundation upon which the credibility of your message will rest.

That is the nature of the gospel. The life of Christ and the demonstration of his love for us at the cross brings power to the message he left with us. If Jesus had not come to live with us or if he had stayed in the grave, the message of the Bible would be anemic at best. But he lived among us, he rose from the dead, and his life is the foundation for the power of his Word.

The same is true as you communicate the gospel to your audience. A group of teenagers will learn more about patience watching their youth leader caught behind a slow driver than they would from a thousand speeches on the subject. Your ability to practice what you preach brings power to what you preach. You can talk to your children about love every day of your life, but the love you demonstrate toward your spouse will ignite your message in their hearts more than all the words in the universe could do alone. A congregation will understand the pastor's message on unconditional love in proportion to his demonstration of that love to difficult members of the congregation.

Itinerant speakers have little opportunity to demonstrate the moral character behind their message. They must take advantage of brief encounters to show that the love of which they speak is at work in their own lives.

Pastors, youth workers, and Sunday school teachers are providing a constant message with their lives. If that message is inconsistent with the message that they preach, then the power of their communication is greatly diminished. If your actions contradict what you say, your actions will speak louder than your words. However, when your actions are consistent with your words, they work together to form the most powerful kind of communication there is.

THE EFFECTIVE COMMUNICATOR
SPEAKS WITH PASSION

A passion for sharing the message of the gospel is also part of the *ethos* that aids communication. There is an enthusiasm that accompanies the message of a speaker who deeply believes the message.

At a large trade show I had occasion to observe two people demonstrate a food processor. I saw the first person do the demonstration just as I entered the building. His sales patter was filled with humor, and he made good use of audience participation. Although the demonstration was interesting, several people, including me, drifted away about halfway through.

I wouldn't even have thought any more about it if I hadn't had to pass this same spot on my way out. A new person was doing the demonstration and this person held the entire crowd until the very end. I waited while he filled several orders because I wanted to congratulate him on his enthusiastic presentation. He had used the same sales talk, but his added enthusiasm and sparkle made all the difference in the world. As we talked, I discovered the reason for his excitement. He was the inventor of the processor and owner of the company. The first person who gave the presentation was only doing his job, but the inventor believed in his product and enjoyed showing others how it worked.

That same kind of passion shows through when you present the gospel. If you believe in it and love sharing it with others, people will be able to tell.

We've all had the experience of listening to preachers who were like these two salesmen. Some preachers just seem to be "doing their jobs." What a difference it makes to sit at the feet of teachers or preachers who are excited about their message! They hold your attention, and you listen to what they are saying because you know they believe it. This kind of enthusiasm is difficult to fake and is almost impossible to hide. Not even the wonderful techniques of preparation and delivery covered in this book can substitute for a vibrant daily relationship with the author of our message. There is such an obvious difference between the speaker who searches for messages because it is his job to deliver them and the speaker who can hardly wait to share what he is learning about the God he loves and lives for daily.

THE EFFECTIVE COMMUNICATOR
CARES ABOUT THE AUDIENCE

A third aspect of this *ethos* is a loving concern for people. People who know that they are loved by a speaker will overlook many faults in style and delivery.

It is easy to seek personal gratification from the audience and forget you are there to serve them. For many years I sought out the laughter and response of my audiences for personal satisfaction. If they didn't respond to my message I would get angry. What a rotten audience, I would think. Once I discovered that my personal worth is not grounded in applause or laughter, it changed my whole approach to preaching, teaching, and entertaining. I am there to give, not to get.

It is a heady experience to be able to hold the attention of an audience. You can use the audience selfishly to feed your ego, or you can choose to allow God to meet the needs of those who hear you through a clear and caring presentation of the Word of God. When you care, it shows. A genuine love for the people to whom you speak will enhance the power of your communication.

THE EFFECTIVE COMMUNICATOR TOUCHES THE EMOTIONS OF THE AUDIENCE

The *pathos* of which Aristotle spoke was the ability to move the audience emotionally. *Pathos* does not refer to manipulative toying with people's emotions. It has to do with personalizing the message so an audience can respond.

Educators acknowledge that three specific learning domains closely parallel Aristotle's statement. These are represented in Figure 1.

The *cognitive* domain is what we know. It is the sterile accumulation of facts. The *affective* domain is what we

LEARNING DOMAINS

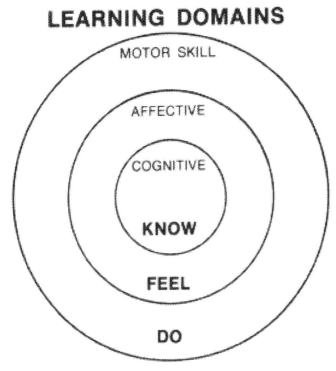

MOTOR SKILL

AFFECTIVE

COGNITIVE

KNOW

FEEL

DO

Figure 1

feel. This domain can be accessed through truth or with lies. It can also be manipulated as an end in itself. The *motor* domain is accessed by action.

It is very easy to concentrate on any one of these domains at the expense of the others. A good storyteller can use the emotion of a story to move people's feelings without an underlying foundation of truth from God's Word. Without that foundation people will quickly abandon whatever they have heard when the feelings have gone.

An academic may find herself simply relaying great amounts of information in the mistaken belief that people will respond to raw data because she does. This kind of "cognitive dump" leaves the majority of the audience cold and unmoved. Finally, the activist will always have his audience doing something.

The best learning takes place when the teacher accesses all three domains. The most effective communication takes place when there is a balance of information (cognitive, know) brought to life with illustration (affective, feel) and personalized with application (motor, do).

A careful study of the ministry of Jesus reveals that he touched people emotionally. People responded strongly to his personal delivery of the truth. Some hated him, some loved him, but few ignored him. Some believed and others decided that he was of the devil and should be killed.

He was presenting the most important cognitive truth in history. This truth had existed in the prophetic writings for years, but his pathos, his personal delivery, and his application of that truth left no room for people to sit idly by.

If you wish to communicate the gospel effectively, you will have to do more than just dump information on the audience or pepper the forest with theological buckshot. Your message is more than a message to be heard, it is a message to be felt and lived. If you are to be effective, your teaching and preaching must touch the emotions of your audience.

THE EFFECTIVE COMMUNICATOR TOUCHES THE
LIVES OF THE AUDIENCE

The last important aspect of your communication is your ability to touch the lives of your audience.

As an itinerant speaker I often hear pastors, youth workers, and volunteers say how they wished they could be in my line of work. They seem to feel that because I have been on television and radio and speak to large numbers of people, somehow my communication is more effective. I believe that is not true. The most effective communicator is one who can live with and touch his or her audience on a day by day basis.

When I was in youth work in northern Minnesota this truth was burned into my heart forever. For several months we had been working with a teenager named Lisa. Although she had heard the gospel message dozens of times she continued to resist giving her life to Christ.

One night my wife, Diane, announced that we were going to a play in which Lisa had a small part. She felt that it was important for us to encourage her and show that we cared by being there. Because I was tired I fought this decision with stern determination. I reasoned that since Lisa had only one or two lines in the entire play, she wouldn't care if we attended. I lost the argument and with a grudging attitude drove to the play. On the way Diane insisted we stop to get some flowers for Lisa. We purchased a half dozen roses, but I made it clear to everyone near me that I was not happy. The play went without a hitch, and Lisa did her few lines with enthusiasm. I was

217

still smoldering when Diane fanned the flames to life by insisting that we go backstage and give Lisa the flowers.

When she saw us standing backstage she was ecstatic. "What did you think?" she bubbled. "Did I do okay?"

We assured her that she was marvelous, and then I remembered the slightly wilted flowers that I was holding behind my back. "Here," I said clumsily, "these are for you."

I will never forget what happened next. Lisa's mouth dropped open as she took the flowers and slowly sank to the floor. With tears streaming down her cheeks she thanked us for coming to her play. "I thought that no one would come because I had such a small part," she cried.

Of course, I felt terrible and the "I told you so" glance from my wife made it even worse. I asked for God's forgiveness that night, but the following week he gave me a gift that was even greater. Lisa came to our home and prayed to receive Christ. If you try to tell me that her decision had nothing to do with a backstage visit and six wilted roses I will disagree.

When you attend a play or basketball game or sit in the home of one who is working through a family crisis, it puts your message in an entirely new light. For those you have touched with your life, your message is clearer and more personal than ever before. Being at the bedside of a sick teenager or playing softball with adults Saturday afternoon makes you more than just the man or woman who gives a talk every week. It makes you a minister, a true communicator of a beautiful message.

My daughters are not impressed by fancy programs and articulate speakers. They have been around both all their lives. If they respond to the message of the gospel, it will be because they are touched by the love of Christ as it is demonstrated in the lives of the men and women who work with them. Likewise, the teachers and speakers who had the greatest influence on me were those who touched me with their lives by their personal involvement.

Speak with clarity and power. Model the message with your life and never stop touching the lives of those to whom you minister. Those characteristics coupled with the techniques of dynamic communication will raise the level of your communication to its fullest potential.

OTHER SERVICES AND MATERIALS AVAILABLE FROM KEN DAVIS

Personal Appearances

Ken Davis is one of the most sought-after communicators in North America. His performances are a unique combination of side-splitting humor and a solid gospel challenge. Ken has appeared on television and stage around the world. His energetic style and expert use of humor reaches people of all ages and backgrounds.

An evening with Ken Davis will definitely make you smile. It may also change your life. For more information…www.kendavis.com.

Speaking Workshops

Ken Davis' Dynamic Communicators Workshops extend a hand to those who want to develop their speaking skills. No matter what your present experience level, these workshops are guaranteed to help you prepare and deliver powerful messages.

Workshop faculty from across the United States represents the top of the communication field. They also share the common attitudes of care and concern that will inspire you to develop your speaking skills.

For further information and a free brochure, write or call:

Dynamic Communicators Workshops
P.O. Box 681568
Franklin, TN 37068-1568
(615) 599-8955

For the most up to date information on Ken Davis' videos, books, audios and other training resources, please visit www.kendavis.com.

Authorized Site and Use License

Definitions

The "Licensed Property" is the *Christian Life School of Theology Global* course contents and delivery systems, hereafter referred to as "Curriculum." The "Owner" of the Curriculum is Christian Life School of Theology Global and is protected by United States and foreign copyright and other intellectual property laws. The "Authorized Site Licensee" is the party or representative of the party entering into this agreement with CLST Global. An "Authorized User" is any staff member of the Licensee, authorized representative, Locally Authorized Teacher, or student using any or all elements of the Licensed Property. The "Site" is the CLEN member school, its programs and students. The "Site" may also be an individual Distance Education student entering into this agreement.

Agreement

Christian Life School of Theology Global hereby grants to the designated Authorized Site Licensee, and the Licensee hereby accepts, a personal, non-exclusive, revocable, non-transferable License to access and use the Curriculum subject to the terms and conditions set forth herein. CLST Global grants to the Licensee and/or all Authorized Users a license to use the Curriculum at the Licensee's Site. All prior agreements, representations, and communications relating to the same subject are superseded by this Agreement. This Agreement may not be modified other than by a written document signed by an authorized representative of each party.

Terms

The Licensed Property may only be used for purposes of education or other non-commercial use. Content will not be used or shared outside of the Licensees' Site. This agreement does not permit anyone other than Authorized Users to use the Curriculum nor permit Authorized Users to use the Curriculum for any uses other than Authorized Uses. Licensee shall not use, or authorize or permit any Student or Staff to use, the Curriculum for any other purpose or in any other manner. The Licensee shall not use the Curriculum for commercial purposes, including but not limited to sale of the Curriculum or bulk reproduction or distribution of the Curriculum, or any portion thereof, in any form. The Licensee may not sell, lend, lease, rent, assign, or transfer the Curriculum to another party in any form. The Licensee may not translate, disassemble, or create derivative works based upon the Curriculum or any part thereof, without the written permission of CLST Global. The Licensee shall make reasonable efforts to prevent Unauthorized Uses of the Licensed Property.

75481713R00126

Made in the USA
San Bernardino, CA
30 April 2018